INTERPERSONAL ACCOUNTS

Social Psychology and Society
General Editors: Howard Giles and Miles Hewstone

Children and Prejudice
Frances Aboud

Contact and Conflict in Intergroup Encounters
Edited by Miles Hewstone and Rupert Brown

Interpersonal Accounts
John H. Harvey, Ann L. Weber, and Terri L. Orbuch

INTERPERSONAL ACCOUNTS

A SOCIAL PSYCHOLOGICAL PERSPECTIVE

John H. Harvey, Ann L. Weber,
and Terri L. Orbuch

Basil Blackwell

Copyright © John H. Harvey, Ann L. Weber, and Terri L. Orbuch 1990

First published 1990

Basil Blackwell, Inc.
3 Cambridge Center
Cambridge, Massachusetts 02142, USA

Basil Blackwell Ltd
108 Cowley Road, Oxford, OX4 1JF, UK

Library of Congress Cataloging in Publication Data

Harvey, John H., 1943–
    Interpersonal accounts: a social psychology perspective/John H. Harvey, Ann L. Weber, and Terri L. Orbuch.
        p.   cm.
    Includes bibliographical references
    ISBN 0–631–17592–X
    1. Interpersonal relations. 2. Interpersonal communication.
    3. Life change events—Psychological aspects.   I. Weber, Ann L.
    II. Orbuch, Terri.   III. Title.
    HM132.H346   1990
    302—dc20   90–31565
                                                              CIP

British Library Cataloguing in Publication Data

A CIP catalogue record for this book is available from the British Library.

Typeset in 10½ on 12pt Times and Univer light by TecSet Ltd, Wallington, Surrey.
Printed in Great Britain by Billing and Sons Ltd, Worcester

Contents

This book is dedicated to the corps of account-makers headed by Victor Frankl who, through their writings, born out of great suffering and anguish, have revealed the merit of the account in enhancing human will and hope; and to our loved ones who have nurtured us in our account-making activity and have helped us appreciate its inestimable value in our lives.

Editor's Preface

Social psychology has, somewhat belatedly, come to recognize the importance of close, long-term relationships between individuals. One of the most significant aspects of behaviour within such relationships is that people frequently "account" for their own and other people's actions. These accounts – meanings organized into a story – are the topic of this, the third book in our series.

Research has shown that accounts are especially likely to be "told", and developed, after the loss of close relationships. They may help people make sense of the loss of these relationships, release emotions and provide a greater sense of psychological control concerning the loss. Accounts do not merely explain events, they also rationalize, justify and help the person to work through grief.

In this volume John Harvey, Ann Weber and Terri Orbuch recognize that accounts play a much wider role in our lives. They provide the most detailed and wide-ranging treatment of accounts to date. They also offer a basic framework within which accounts can be understood, and they draw on the varieties of specialist literatures now dealing with the topic. They go on to demonstrate the role of account-making in response to severe stress, how we perceive other persons, and how we deal with perhaps the most traumatic aspect of any relationship – bereavement. They argue, provocatively, for the evolutionary significance of account-making and for a focus on literary, as well as more traditional, sources of data for social-psychological research.

This volume succeeds admirably in one of the aims of our series – namely, to disseminate the ideas of social psychology to other disciplines. This book will be of interest to scholars and students in health psychology, communication, family studies, bereavement and related areas, as well as to those working in more traditional domains such as attribution theory and interpersonal relations. It is also of obvious applied relevance – concerning how people make sense of and cope with major issues in their lives, such as conflict in close relationships, life transitions (job loss, retirement) and a host of other stressful events. Finally, the book provides a highly accessible summary of current thinking on the topic of accounts; it will surely, as is its aim, stimulate further thinking and research on this important issue.

Howard Giles and Miles Hewstone

Preface

This book is aimed at providing a scholarly treatment of accounts and account-making, principally as social psychological phenomena. It is directed toward courses in social and health psychology, communication studies, family studies, and related fields, focusing on how people make sense of, and cope with, major issues in their lives, such as close relationships conflict and dissolution; transition in one's life, as in losing a job in retirement; death of a loved one; or other such stressful events and dilemmas. Our work is also directed toward general audiences who appreciate the value and impact of stories and story-telling in our lives.

As the reader will see, our sampling of literature is diverse in nature – from scholarly journal articles to poetry, novels, and short stories, and best of all from ordinary people's own accounts about matters of moment to them.

This book has a number of roots, which will be traced more fully in chapter 1. One course is our collective passion for, and belief in, the value of the topic of this book for contemporary social psychology, as well as other areas of the social and behavioural sciences. As Myerhoff (1978) has suggested, our species is best dubbed *homo narrans*, humankind as story-teller. Humans frequently search for meaning, even if at times in implicit and unconscious ways. We believe that it is in their accounts about issues and problems of importance in their lives that this search process is most intense, prolonged, and sometimes agonizing. Given that view, in this book, we wish to provide a better foundation for theoretical analysis and research on accounts and the account-making process.

A more practical wellspring for this volume was the stimulus of the First International Conference on Personal Relationships in 1982 at Madison, Wisconsin. This conference was developed and co-ordinated by two of the foremost pioneering psychologists in the relationship field, Steve Duck and Robin Gilmour. At that conference, the first two authors were invited to give a talk summarizing our recent work on close relationships. The direction we decided to take, however, was somewhat different from that presented in earlier works on the role of attribution in the termination of close relationships (Harvey, Wells, and Alvarez, 1978; Harvey, Weber, Yarkin, and Stewart, 1982). Until then, most attribution-relationship work had focused on attributions as relatively singular interpretations made by persons in relationships about relationship events and their partners. We, however, wanted to broaden this focus to consider both theoretically and empirically much more of the "story-like" interpretations people naturalistically provide about their most compelling relationships dilemmas. In this book we call these stories *accounts*.

The topic of our invited talk at Madison was on the "special case of the account" in the termination process. Such a topic had been suggested by Weiss (1975) in his provocative analysis of the role of the account in psychological repair following marital separation. Harvey, Wells, and Alvarez (1978) began to introduce this term to the attribution literature and reported a small amount of accounts evidence provided by newly separated persons in the form of diaries. At the 1982 meeting, Harvey and Weber began to extend this idea far beyond its initial scope and to develop more theoretical clarity and stature. We focused on its functions, determinants, and consequences, and possible significance in the psychology of close relationships, resulting in a modest theoretical paper (Harvey, Weber, Galvin, Huszti and Garnick, 1986).

The real substance of illustrative evidence for this paper was not Weiss's reports of accounts, but rather the reports of persons who had engaged in extramarital affairs (Hunt, 1969), an assortment of short-story and novel material compiled by Weber, and finally, the comments of a young woman who obliged us with her account while sitting on a bench on State Street in Madison. It was a pot-pourri of "data," to say the least. But the key for the present work is that all of these types of illustration of accounts were inspiring of further work. The conference participants generally were receptive to these ideas, and the accounts topic has begun to occupy an "in the wings" position over these years, in terms of its potential to help scholars understand people's interpretive and coping activities in the face of troubling personal events. Among the most perceptive and helpful attendees then and at later conferences in which Weber and Harvey made presentations was Orbuch, our third author. While Harvey and Weber are social psychologists from the psychological side,

Orbuch is a social psychologist from the sociological side. She provides a helpful, broad perspective for this work on accounts, and she was in charge of the beginning of a research program on person perception and accounts, which is summarized in this volume.

After these developments and our publication of several works on accounts (Weber, Stanley, and Harvey, 1987; Harvey, Turnquist, and Agostinelli, 1988; Harvey, Agostinelli, and Weber, 1989; Harvey, Orbuch, and Weber, 1990), we believe that the time is ripe for a monograph-length treatment of our conception of accounts and what we have called the account-making process (that is, the psychological and social steps leading to an individual's production of an account). Our aim is to stimulate thinking, writing, and research on this topic. Increasingly, the topic is gaining credence among a broad circuit of social and behavioural scientists. We believe the timing of this monograph is also propitious because it follows some pertinent and useful edited books that have recently been published (e.g. Burnett, McGhee, and Clarke, 1987; Antaki, 1988).

In short, the accounts area is an exciting new one for theory and research progress. We also realize that many related literatures and relevant writings may have been neglected by us. In part, this neglect reflects the potential breadth of our topic. We do sincerely apologize to other scholars who have dealt with similar concepts, whose writings are not acknowledged in this book.

As the reader will see, we believe that account-making plays a vital role in a stress-response sequence, which applies to many phenomena, including, but hardly restricted to, psychological events occurring in the wake of relationship loss. In effect, we are beginning to extend our ideas to encompass reactions to more general forms of major loss and trauma. Now, we are beginning to make a case for the status of account-making and accounts as much more critical to human adaptation than has been previously recognized. The reader will be the judge of the case that we present; we welcome that scrutiny. Others may also come to cherish the preciousness of these human stories we tell in and after our seasons of deepest anguish.

John H. Harvey
Ann L. Weber
Terri L. Orbuch

February, 1990

Acknowledgements

We wish to express our deepest appreciation to a number of people who have greatly facilitated our work as represented in this volume. We thank Steve Duck and Robin Gilmour who, as organizers of the First International Conference on Personal Relationships in 1982, initially gave us the opportunity to begin the process of studying account-making. Steve Duck deserves special gratitude for continuing to support our work and for providing a further forum for our ideas at the 1988 Iowa Network on Personal Relationships Workshop, which focused on accounts. We are most grateful to Harold Kelley, Jud Mills, and Ellen Berscheid who have provided special support along the way as our ideas have been nurtured and revised. Our editors of this Blackwell series, Howard Giles and Miles Hewstone, also deserve strong praise. Howard's enthusiasm for our project meant a lot to us when we began the process of seeking a publisher, and we benefited greatly from his earlier commentary on our work as represented in a paper published by the *Journal of Language and Social Psychology*, a journal that Howard edits. Miles provided an excellent commentary on a draft of the book. Among other revisions based on his evaluation, his comments led us to revise substantially chapter 4 and to develop the theoretical conception of account-making and person perception found in that chapter. Our editors at Blackwell, particularly Philip Carpenter, Kim DiDonato, Ruth Kimber, Andrew McNeillie, and Leigh Peake, have taken good care of us in the negotiation and editorial processes.

We are grateful to our many colleagues who contributed intellectually to the germination of our ideas about account-making. These include Mara Adelman, Gina Agostinelli, Charles Antaki, Mary Burgess, Kathryn Galvin, Fritz and Grace Heider, Clyde and Susan Hendrick, Heather Huszti, Kris Pond, Dawn Roberts, Shauna Russell, Melinda Stanley, Robert Stewart, and Giffold Weary. Lest we forget, we owe thanks to the many research participants who have shared with us many intimate details of their lives. Finally, we thank Becky Huber and Gail Garwood who made helpful contributions to the production of the book. In the end, of course, we take full responsibility for what is written.

The authors and publishers wish to thank the following for permission to use copyright material: Houghton Mifflin Company for material from *The Origin of Consciousness in the Breakdown of the Bicameral Mind* by Julian Jaynes. Copyright © 1976 by Julian James; North Point Press for 'A Life' by Dan Pagis excerpted from *Variable Directions*, originally published in the *New Yorker*. Copyright © 1989 by Stephen Mitchell (translator); Random House, Inc. Alfred A. Knopf, Inc. for an excerpt from *Breathing Lessons* by Anne Tyler, Alfred A. Knopf. Copyright © 1988 by AMT, Inc.; and 'The Poem by Dusty' from *Shrapnel in the Heart* by Laura Palmer, Random House, Inc. Copyright © 1987 by Laura Palmer; University Press of New England for 'The Snapshots' and 'Brief Song' from *Sam's Book* by David Ray. Copyright © 1987 by David Ray; Warner Chappell Music Ltd. and Warner Chappell Music, Inc. for 'The Last Time I Saw Richard' (Joni Mitchell). Copyright © 1971, 1975 Joni Mitchell Publishing Corp.

Part I
Foundations for Theory and Research in Account-making

In these chapters, we describe the conceptual and empirical bases for work on accounts and account-making. Chapter 1 describes our own beginnings in theoretical work in articulating the motivations and conditions for account-making. Chapter 2 provides a review of work on accounts in popular and scholarly literature. Chapter 3 presents a conception of account-making under conditions of severe stress, and chapter 4 describes early work on a research program designed to examine the link between person perception and account-making – how are people who present different kinds of accounts perceived by others?

1   Introduction: Basic Framework

O, what a world of unseen visions and heard silences, this insubstantial country of the mind! What ineffable essences, these touchless rememberings and unshowable reveries! And the privacy of it all! A secret theater of speechless monologue and prevenient counsel, an invisible mansion of all moods, musings, and mysteries, an infinite resort of disappointments and discoveres.

Julian Jaynes, 1976

Without a fall off from perfection, there can be no story-telling.

Anonymous

You cannot tell people what to do. You can only tell them parables.

W. H. Auden

As adults, humans possess vast repositories of stories, each filled with images, feelings, actors, plots, and lines. These stories may be fragmented, or they may become fragmented in our memories as we age. Nevertheless, taken together, they represent part of the immense psychic landscape that makes us symbolic creatures in our essence. Along with many other commentators on the human condition (e.g. Frankl, 1963), we believe that people are inexorably driven to search for meaning in their own and their significant others' personal histories. This book is about these stories, which we call accounts, and the process whereby they are developed and become part of our mental life and behavioral plans and patterns.

In 1977, George Levinger concluded a perceptive essay on close relationships by suggesting that a principal reason for relationship dilemmas (with a divorce trend in the United States then approaching its highest point) might be people's inarticulateness in addressing issues in their relationships. Indeed, that conclusion may be well taken and tenable today. A premise of this book, however, is that whether or not verbalized to their close others, people regularly – and sometimes incessantly and to no end – are looking for an understanding of the major issues in their lives – which may or may not concern their close others. It is that quest for understanding and meaning, which may go on in subtle, almost unconscious ways, that is at the heart of account-making.

DEFINITION, SCOPE, AND HISTORICAL NOTES

An account is like a story that contains a rich array of plots, characters, and patterns of interaction. It is the package containing explanations and descriptive material for events and states of being of self, other, and the world. The definition we prefer for an account is contained in the first two denotations for "account" in the *Random House Dictionary* (1978): "1. a description of events or facts. 2. an explanatory statement." As we shall discuss in chapter 2, this definition is relatively neutral in valence; other definitions have emphasized the justificatory or excusatory nature of accounts. Our focus is on an account as a story that may contain justifications and other types of self- and other-relevant material. Why not simply say we are studying "stories" and "story-telling" processes? We have no overwhelming reason for rejecting these alternative terms as our primary terms in this analysis. None the less, we prefer the "accounts" and "account-making" concepts because they now have a more clearcut, developing literature in social psychology.

How do we know when an account has started or ended? How do we define the boundaries of an account? We shall discuss methodological issues at the end of this chapter. Here, we shall contend that the boundaries for accounts may be defined either by the participants themselves, using techniques not unlike the thought-listing technique employed in the attitude change area (Petty and Cacioppos, 1986), or by the investigator using contextual information. Gergen and Gergen (1987) discuss the frequent use of "demarcation signs" for people's narrative reports to others. For example, one person may begin a story with, "You can't imagine what happened to me . . . ", and end it with, "So now you know what happened."

We shall argue in chapter 2 that accounts are similar to narratives, except that we contend that accounts may not involve telling one's story to others (that is, they may remain at the level of private reflections or be written for self and/or other to read). Hence, accounts may have boundaries marked by such demarcations. However, our position is that operational definitions of accounts need to be developed in accordance with the theorectical perspective under test; not unlike attributions or emotions or other social psychological constructs, there need be no singularly definitive procedure for learning about accounts. The key emphasis, in our view, is on the overall story, or Gestalt, contained in the account. Thus, in this Gestalt metaphor, an account is more than the sum of its individual attributions. The process of composing the account may continue for many years, or may be completed in short order.

Work on accounts has a number of historical roots, some of which will be traced more fully in the next chapter. The concept was first introduced by the sociologists (reviewed in chapter 2) who discussed accounts in terms of excuses people make when they are associated with potentially culpable behavior. These scholars did not give the concept the broad, story-like characterization that we wish to emphasize. In the field of social psychology, work on accounts has developed in close association to theory and research on attributional processes (Heider, 1958; Orvis, Kelley, and Butler, 1976; Harvey, Wells, and Alvarez, 1978). Heider's work, in particular, is a beacon of insight about how people understand one another and achieve coherence in their interpersonal relations. His classic "naive psychology," or "commonsense psychology of the person on the street," represents a metaphor which we believe provides an umbrella for account-making activity and which we shall refer to in our analysis. For example, we shall argue that central to a person's naive psychology is his or her reservoir of stories about self and others (including not only images and memories of real happenings, but imaginations of mentally created events as well) and how those stories are formed, accessed over time, and modified.

The concept of account was first explicitly introduced to psychology by Weiss in his influential book *Marital Separation* (1975). He gave the concept an identity that we find quite congenial in our analysis. He described the importance of an account to recently separated persons and defined it in the following passages:

> For months after the end of the marriage, events leading to its breakdown are likely to occupy the thoughts of the separated husband and wife. Again and again they review what went wrong, justify or regret the actions they took,

consider and reconsider their own words and those of their spouse. Endlessly, they replay actual scenes in their minds or create scenes that did not happen but could have, in which they said different things or took different actions so that the separation was averted or the spouse was told off once and for all.

Gradually the separated come to terms with the events of their marriage. They develop an *account*, a history of the marital failure, a story of what their spouse did and what they did and what happened in consequence. Often the account focuses on a few significant events that dramatize what went wrong, or on a few themes that ran through the marriage; in addition it allocates blame among the self, the spouse, and third parties who may have entered their lives, and so settles the moral issues of the separation.

The account is of major psychological importance to the separated, not only because it settles the issue of who was responsible for what, but also because it imposes on the confused marital events that preceded the separation a plot structure with a beginning, middle, and end and so organizes the events into a conceptually manageable unity. Once understood in this way, the events can be dealt with: They can be seen as outcomes of identifiable causes and, eventually, can be seen as past, over and external to the individual's present self. Those who cannot construct accounts sometimes feel that their perplexity keeps them from detaching themselves from the distressing experiences. (Weiss, 1975, pp. 14–15)

Although Weiss's treatment of the account was restricted to the situation involving marital separation, his analysis strongly suggests that the account-making process may play a restorative role in many types of griefwork after loss. We shall pursue the possibility in a later chapter. We shall also argue, in our presentation of a model of the account-making process in response to severe stress, that this process represents a crucial aspect of effective coping with such stress and in using stressful events to give one's life new purpose and resolve.

BASIC CHARACTERISTICS

As we shall argue later, the account-making process involves several component activities, including the cognitive work of remembering, analyzing, searching one's mind, and the development of subsidary activities such as affective reactions and behavioral expectations. It may also involve discussion with others – soliciting their response to the story, or simply using them as sounding-boards for a monologue. We suggest that accounts are quite similar to photo albums. They are often compartmentalized and help us organize our memories and understanding of important events and eras, and the significant others with whom we were involved as those periods of time unfolded. For example, we may have an account for each "era" in our relationship lives – just as we may have a set of illustrative photographs. That is, accounts may be organized according to our recollection of these significant others and relevant events concerning them, and our interpretation of their meaning in the larger picture of our lives. This organization may be termed the "compartmentalization of accounts." The account-maker may also have an overarching *master account* which subsumes and organizes these more specific accounts. This concept is similar to what Gergen and Gergen (1988) refer to as "macronarrative." The macronarrative refers to a person's overall life-story and may be distinguished from the "micronarrative," which refers to accounts of brief incidents. Throughout our lives, accounts per era/event/partner amass in our memory and may blur across boundaries.

Accounts correspond partially to what Kelley (1983) refers to as perceived causal structure. In Kelley's conception, a perceived causal structure pertains to the networks or chains of causes that people often employ in understanding events. One cause is seen to lead to an effect which itself becomes the cause for a further effect, and so on. Also, several causes may be seen as jointly determining a single effect, or a given cause may give rise to several different effects. Or circular causality may be inferred. Kelley cites as illustrative of the use of perceived causal structures people's accounts for various events, including Fletcher's (1983) report of people's explanations for their marital separation. From our position, the concept of perceived causal structure bears considerable resemblance to that of an account. An important possible difference is that people may initially perceive/understand in terms of these structures and later provide accounts that more or less reflect their initial perceptions of structure. By definition, though, accounts represent the product of the end, or retrospective, stage in the explaining process, while perceived causal structures may come into play either at the beginning or as part of the account-making activity.

Accounts may be sharply etched, dramatic, powerful, highly coherent, and complete. But sometimes they are like meanderings, erratically pieced-together fragments of meaning regarding central events and people on our psychic stages. Yet they are all we have in terms of our own life-stories, or the overall master-story. Hemingway is reported to have said that if stories go on long enough, they all have the same ending – namely, someone's death. Perhaps that is true with accounts and account-making too. But along the way, we suggest that the different themes of different accounts, as well as the different accounts per eras of a person's life, are of consequence. The individual develops an account much as if he or she were searching for hypotheses to fit the data: the best fitting story will "explain" it all, and will become the (current) True Story. For example, an account that maintains that a relationship was "wrong from the start" will have different behavioral implications from one that plays on the theme of "wrong place, wrong time" or "just one of those things." As the individual experiences more than one close relationship, the accounts may begin to accumulate and even exert an influence on each other. Given the time necessary for one to "rack up" such experiences and to gain a perspective on them, we should recognize that these accounts start to pile up in late adolescence and early mid-life and then become fixed in the memory, remaining at some level with us to the grave. Even though we accord much importance to the contents of accounts, we shall argue in this book that it is the *process* of forming the account and the feeling that you have a sufficient account that are most relevant to psychological well-being and direction.

What is the mind attempting to understand in the account-making process? Robert Penn Warren (1989) suggested that a story is not an image of life, but life in motion – specifically the presentation of individual characters moving through their particular experiences, dealing with some conflict or problem, and diligently searching for a resolution. No conflict, no story, argued Warren. Our own work focuses on the mind's quest to understand our major stresses: why doesn't she love me? Why am I so vulnerable to him? Why was my friend taken from this world so suddenly and unjustly? Why did my father abuse me? Why did I commit that act of cruelty to my wife? Why am I so weak and unable to control my emotions when I am with her? "Why me, Lord?"

These questions are important. As each of us lives (and the longer we live), we incur the increasing probability of experiencing divorce, destitution, physical disability, mental depression, great anguish about the death of loved ones, and the certainty of our own death. As we construe meaning, these events call for us to summon our courage to continue and, we would argue, a need to contextualize them within the huge mental array that constitutes our representation of our life-course. At its heart, we argue, such a contextualization involves account-making. In this process, we link the event to such issues as who we are, who we want to be, who we may be becoming, why such events occur in general, and to the future and what the event portends.

A central thesis of this book is that account-making is especially beneficial to the individual trying to come to grips psychologically with major personal loss, and to construe something of value as a consequence of the loss. In her powerful book *Necessary Losses* (1986) Judith Viorst discusses the importance of using the human experience of inevitable loss to stimulate personal growth: "Throughout our life we grow by giving up. We give up some our deepest attachments to others. We give up cherished parts of ourselves . . . Passionate investment leaves us vulnerable to loss. And sometimes, no matter how clever we are, we must lose" (Viorst, 1986, p. 3). David Morrell, author of the *Rambo* series of books, poignantly describes how he tried to come to terms with the sudden death from cancer of his teenage son by writing a semi-autobiographical account of these events in his work *Fireflies* (1988). Morrell indicates that, initially, he wrote the book so that his son would be remembered and also as an informal psychoanalysis for himself. But then, as the appreciative mail poured in from parents who had also lost children, he began to realize the broader contribution of the story of his son, his son's great courage as he suffered, and his own insurmountable grief in response to his son's death. The value of the book thus also lay in its provision of hope for those in such agony of grief. We suggest that in its noblest form, account-making often carries out such a mission in our lives. It helps us cope and find meaning beyond loss, and it helps us give some of that hope and meaning to others who also suffer.

Examples

We shall provide a fuller sampling of types of accounts in a later chapter; for now the following excerpts of accounts are presented as illustrations of what we have in mind when we use this term. The first account (reported in Scarf, 1980) pertains to a 28-year-old woman's reflection on the possible causes of the demise of a long-term relationship; it represents well the relatively common theme of "would not make a commitment:"

> I was more mature, in many ways, than Philip was . . . . It was as if I had, in some way, a stronger sense of who I was . . . and this was, I think, threatening to him. So he would push me away and be rejecting. And yet . . . I always understood. I understood this, and didn't drag him into long hassles about it; I was pretty tolerant . . . . With Philip, though, it was the first time . . . I ever became that involved. And yet it didn't work out. I *knew*, almost at once, that it wouldn't work. (Scarf, 1980, p. 221)

The next examples come from reports made by Vitenam veterans on their difficulty in adjusting to civilian life after the war. These accounts capture the veteran's dismay, confusion, and sense of betrayal by those who had been closest to them and, more generally, by their country. The first comes from an account given by a 40-year-old veteran commenting on his continuing war-related stresses and experiences with his wife and at college upon his return from Vietnam:

> I still can feel the sheer terror. I still have flashes of the scenes of death and dying. Things have a way of reminding you of a situation you encountered there . . . being unable to relax. Sometimes I startle and want to hit the deck when I hear a car backfire. Sometimes I wake up in panic that I can't get my gun loaded fast enough . . . I have a great fear of the unknown.
> I was comfortable before I left for Nam. I had been married for two years and had many good friends. But when I returned, it was as if I had changed greatly and had no control over what I found here. My wife was waiting for me, and soon after returning our relationship started to deteriorate . . . I was in a daze. I didn't know what was going on . . . .
> I encountered hostility when I went back to college. I had no place there. I wasn't much older but I was different . . . and they made me feel that way. And the students were into various kinds of power – brown and black and so on. Before I left and in the service, I didn't encounter such groups; you just had friends regardless of color. I was dealing with kids in college who didn't know anything about what I had experienced or what it was like over there . . . . All that I could communicate with them was second-level bathroom bullshit.
> I wanted to be off by myself and not around anyone – wife, parents, former friends . . . I felt then and still feel today that I can only talk about Nam with other vets who were there . . . I and the vets like me were and still are somewhat totally separate from the rest of the world. (Harvey, Turnquist, and Agostinelli, 1988, p. 38)

The second excerpt comes from another Vietnam veteran who also found that his close relationship was quickly dissolving and that he could not readily relate to family and friends:

> My girlfriend told me she didn't know how to relate to me . . . I had expected things to be the way they were; but they weren't. She said she thought I had been killed in the war, because I stopped writing to her. Honestly, I didn't know how to relate to her now either. I dreaded going to bed with her . . . . She also said that I wasn't the loving guy she used to know and love, that something horrible must have happened to me over there to change me so completely . . . . She said the look in my eyes was the look of a deeply terrorized person, with a long-distance stare . . . . She said that besides, she had found somebody else anyway. That really hurt me . . . .
> When it came to my family, my mother told me that I wasn't as considerate and sweet as I used to be. My dad felt I wasn't as diligent and committed as he

remembered me to be prior to Vietnam. I didn't know what any of these people were saying. I knew I was getting pissed off more and more by hearing all of this bullshit. (Brende and Parson, 1985, p. 46)

THE WHYS OF ACCOUNTS: MOTIVATIONS FOR ACCOUNT-MAKING

We believe that accounts are learned primarily in the same ways that people learn other social behavior: from parents, peers, and the media. It is likely, though, that account-making becomes most pronounced as a way of dealing with the world for the young adult, when this developing person has begun to taste some of life's bitter pills, such as the pain of rejection in dating and social activity, and the crushing blow of defeat in athletic or academic performance. Such experiences compel us to try to understand them because in each domain we want very much to succeed. One of our opening quotations suggests what we shall be emphasizing in this book: that story-telling or account-making derives above all from "a fall from perfection," or more generally, from having to come to grips with difficult, even traumatic, personal circumstances. So what do we do in these circumstances? We turn to explanations provided by others (peers, friends, parents) and by the media. For example, one type of an account might be, "She won't go out with me because she is hung up on six-foot-tall hunks who play in the football team." This helps ease the pain a little and gets us back on our feet to try again. Thus, we learn to develop and refine our explanations in their story form, and we also may learn – tentatively and selectively – to discuss them with others. Increasingly, the present authors believe that much of the contents of our account-making about close relationships are acquired in the "relationship talk" that we participate in and that we overhear in conversations among our friends and family, and on the television. Further, it appears that women engage in such talk more intensively and regularly than do men (see the discussion of relevant research by Holtzworth-Munroe and Jacobson, 1985, p. 18 below). Men, too, sometimes engage in this sort of talk (and may be changing over time to do so more); and even if they do not do so, they are likely to engage in degrees of "relationship-think" as regularly as women engage in this more private account-making. In a similar way, it seems that both men and women learn how to talk about other kinds of dilemma and trauma in their lives directly and vicariously from those who have experienced such difficulties.

More specifically, in our work, we have identified a set of motivations of accounts that includes: enhancement of feelings of control and clarification of understanding, self-esteem maintenance and enhancement, emotional purging, the search for closure and as an end in themselves, and an enlightened feeling and an enhanced will and hope. We shall treat each one of these motivations below.

Quest for Control and Understanding

As will be discussed more fully in chapter 2, the concept of account has been introduced in a variety of contexts by different scholars in the behavioral sciences. Weiss (1975) first discussed the value of accounts for the grieving married person who had recently experienced marital separation. A principal motivation of the newly separate individual in trying to cope with the emotion and loss is to gain a greater sense of understanding of why the relationship ended and of personal control over the situation and the future. To some degree, this type of account-making is like "Monday morning quarterbacking" (i.e., after the fact, to think that an outcome should have been anticipated if one were rationally processing information). Events that seemed to offer little coherence during their unfolding now seem more understandable: "I should have guessed all along that he was seeing someone else. How could I have been so stupid?" Even if such lines sound like old refrains in our world, as part of fuller stories they help give the account-maker a greater sense of understanding of a traumatic event and also a perception that in the future he or she will have more control *because of* this greater understanding. The actor–account-maker, in short, is always more in control than the actor who does not have an account available. The actor should feel more in control of personal events to the extent that he or she has a repertoire of accounts for the types of events being experienced. This reasoning is somewhat similar to that found in scheme theory, which suggests that schema help us feel that we have more control and predictability in our lives (e.g. Markus, 1977; Fiske and Taylor, 1984). It should be noted that accounts often contain many schemata (for example, about the self) which are ways of organizing knowledge or experience. Thus, this control motivation in account-making is central to the growth of the individual as a social being. We have to become story-tellers to know that we can face with more confidence and resolve the future and its many perils for our happiness.

In the next section, we discuss the importance of account-making for one's self-esteem. Self-insight and a sense of personal control also contribute positively to self-esteem. These related feelings may be stimulated by the account-maker's effort in keeping a personal diary. As Jeanne Schinto (1987) suggests, in discussing the value of her own diary of her teenage years, "Seeing my diaries in the context of lives similar to my own, then, I understand much better how I am part of a historical picture – a genre, a movement, a trend – and I can step back and appreciate more objectively, less self-consciously, the value of things such as high school conversations I recorded verbatim" ("Private Lives," *The Boston Globe Magazine*, November 8, 1987, p. 38).

Self-esteem Maintenance and Enhancement

Self-esteem is a fragile commodity in our lives as social beings. It is so easily damaged, sometimes almost beyond repair. We, therefore, exhibit a lot of effort and spend a lot of time simply trying to hold constant or bolster our sense of self-worth. Sometimes we do so via the accounts we tell ourselves and others. As Cross (1986) suggests, people often gain a greater sense of personal importance in the world by fitting events they observe into stories they know. She also notes the power conveyed to the writer or diarist of the story: "until she . . . writes down whatever happened, turns it into a story, it hasn't really happened, it hasn't shape, form, reality. I think so many women keep diaries and journals in the hope of giving some shape to their inchoate lives" (Cross, 1986, p. 35).

We argue that the account-maker often presents his or her accounts both to others in conversation and writing, and to self via private reflections in a way designed to enhance or protect self-esteem. We do not necessarily distinguish between private and public self-esteem, as has been done in the attribution literature (Weary and Arkin, 1981). Jones and Pittman (1982) cogently theorize about various presentation tactics that people use in different situations. For example, people may ingratiate themselves with others; sometimes they self-promote; or they are supplicants, and so on. In each of these tactical presentations, the personal story may be a key aspect of the strategy. A man may tell a prospective new lover that his wife left him and their good marriage because of her need to experience new relationships. In telling this story, he may suggest to the potential lover that he would be a good lover who would not be unfaithful, and he may imply that he needs her to ease this undeserved pain. Similarly, a woman reporting to a male friend that "I'd say to myself, 'My husband is right. I'm sure a terrible person. I'm such a bitch . . . no one will ever want me again . . . '" may in effect be soliciting the male friend's affections so as to dissuade herself from the view that she will never have another lover.

While there is a glaring paucity of research on this interface of self-presentation and account-making, our reasoning here suggests that people frequently select a particular account depending on who is listening. The audience's receptiveness and reaction must be anticipated and the reported account tailored accordingly. A same-sex friend, for example, may elicit an account that blames other and exonerates self. Weiss (1975) notes that after a separation, members of a parting couple may have to agree on who gets "custody" of which friends. On the other hand, an opposite-sex potential lover may elicit a mixture of self-promotion and supplication because the account-maker is not sure which presentation will be the better received.

A further interesting implication of this argument is that an account-maker may frequently be confused as to the truth of any particular account – one may have presented so many different versions that one has now forgotten the story first believed most strongly. In fact, consistent with Daryl Bem's (1972) intriguing self-perception analysis, we may expect that people sometimes come to believe their publicly reported accounts, which were initially presented quite hesitantly. That is, in certain circumstances, "saying is believing." From the perspective of psychobiography, Runyan (1982) has suggested that there is no such thing as a definitive biography. Lives are exceedingly complex, and many different perspectives can be brought to bear in reporting on any one life. This view seems especially tenable when considering a person's account of his or her own life. As we shall describe more fully in chapter 3, the possibility of cognitive or motivated distortion and bias in memory is particularly strong in the act of recalling one's own life-events.

Whether or not it is considered to be true by the account-maker, the reported account will almost always be designed to have an enhancing or restorative effect on self-worth. Mead (1934) argued that the social mind is the assimiliation within the individual of the social process. The individual takes the role of other and reacts as other would (should) and, in so doing, the individual shares the perception of other. We believe that, even if only in fragments, accounts are usually reported to others over time; the social affirmation/feedback process for our thoughts and feelings is too persuasive and powerful for most humans to avoid fully.

Emotional Purging

People sometimes use accounts to experience catharsis, or purge themselves, of unpleasant emotional states that have built up in the grieving process. The best example of this motivation is provided in Rosenblatt's (1983) *Bitter, Bitter Tears*. In this book, he presents a searching analysis of griefwork among nineteenth-century diarists whose thoughts and feelings have been elicited from their personal diaries. Separation during this century often occurred as a result of a loved one's migration in search of work, or as a result of early death due to disease. Grieving in the form of diary-reporting probably relieves the individual of part of the continuing emotional attachment to the lost loved one – that is, it facilitates the natural detachment process. In another sense, it helps dull the pain and ease the burden. (It may even help the account-maker feel less responsible or guilty for the loss – whether or not responsibility or guilt are in anyway appropriate.) Unlike account-making relevant to self-esteem, it would appear that emotional purging is undertaken to relieve oneself of emotional pain. Account-making in bereavement, therefore, is not a self-presentation whose primary concern is audience reaction. It is, in short, a pure form of grieving and releasing or letting go.

Music or the lyrics of songs are often related to the cathartic function of account-making (as well as to many of the other functions discussed here). As an illustration, the singer Judy Collins reports that she became a singer because she loves to tell stories and that she has kept a diary for over twenty years as "a healing device" (reported in *USA Today*, 24 November, 1987, in Collins' comments about her book *Trust Your Heart* (1987) which sprang from her diary). Songwriters who write "Country and Western" lyrics are particularly adroit at developing story-lines that speak to people's needs to vent feelings about romantic loss and hurt. Randy Owen, the lead singer of the group Alabama, recalled the events that stimulated his writing of the song "Lady Down on Love":

> It was at a motel lounge in Bowling Green, Kentucky. Between sets we stopped to talk with some of the people, "What brings you out tonight?" he asked a table of women. "We're celebrating her divorce," one replied. I asked her, "Are you happy about it?" She said, "Not really. I'd rather be at home and in love with my husband." That struck me.
>
> She said it was the first time she'd been out on the town since she was 18 years old. That's where that line in the song comes from. I went back to my room and wrote it in 15 minutes. (Interview, *The Nashville Tennessean*, 15 January, 1985, p.5d)

The Search for Closure: The Account as an End in Itself

Another motivation for account-making is that of the combined goal of seeking mental closure on a chain of events, or simply as an end in itself. As Weber, Harvey, and Stanley (1987) argue, the importance of closure cannot be underestimated in terms of psychological tranquility. Closure, an important Gestalt principle, suggests that we feel ill-at-ease if a story is left unfinished – a principle that has been dubbed the *Zeigarnik Effect*. In the late 1920s, Bluma Zeigarnik demonstrated that individuals who were prevented from finishing stories they had been reading had a greater and more detailed recall of those stories than did individuals who had been allowed to finish reading (Zeigarnik, 1938). In essence, those who had finished reading their stories mentally filed them away and forgot about them. According to the Zeigarnik Effect, we are disturbed by loose ends; we do not like not knowing how something turned out.

Consider this process as it pertains to close relationships. Developing and relating to our own accounts of our relational experiences allows us to tie up any loose ends that might have been left hanging. Closure in accounts may provide the stability we need and seek, yet which proves so elusive in relationships themselves. Closure in our accounts may be the only kind of closure we can successfully obtain and realize at the time. Closure becomes a sort of Holy Grail: we always seek it; we are not satisfied until we have reached it in some form. Perhaps, aspects of account-making are even more satisfying than certain aspects of the real relationship. An account gives us closure not only in "documenting" *how* a relationship ended, but in fact *that* the relationship ended. Relatedly, an account mayu be *an end in itself*. The account is, after all, the lone vestige of the close relationship now gone. All we have left are our stories, mental images, and memories; perhaps all we ever had are our stories, a suggestion made by Alice Koller (1981) in the course of her own poignant, searching self-analysis. Harvey et al. (1982) argue that close personal relationships do *not* end; rather they continue, albeit at the cognitive and emotional level, rather than in day-to-day interaction and experience: "Relationships are as much symbolic events and images to the involved parties as they are interactional episodes or histories. We may put spaces or time or other people between ourselves and formerly significant others, but we maintain the relationships in our mind" (Harvey et al., 1982, p. 119).

Enlightened Feeling and Enhanced Will and Hope

Accounts may be told and re-told over time because they enlighten and give the account-maker the will and hope to continue. This motive may be seen as superordinate to the other motives discussed above. For example, it subsumes and is different from emotional purging because it strongly represents a positive, uplifting experience, while purging may represent above all a release of negative feelings toward others or the central event. It also subsumes and is different from ego-enhancement, since it involves a broader motivation – that might involve a desire to contribute to others in a relatively selfless way. The anthropologist Barbara Myerhoff, in *Number Our Days* (1978), provides a penetrating report and analysis of the lives and struggles of a group of elderly Jewish immigrants living in Los Angeles. She relates how they regularly tell stories of their former lives as a way of giving continuity to their shared cultural traditions and belief systems. To us, this activity appears to represent well the motivation of enlightened feeling and enhanced will and hope. Myerhoff concludes her book with the observation that humans basically are *homo narrans*, humankind as story-teller. By this phrase, she seems to imply that in any culture the very fabric of meaning that constitutes every person's existence is the "story" we tell about ourselves. One of her respondents reflects the uplifting nature of story-telling as he imagined the many loved ones he had lost as a result of the Nazi atrocities:

> But finally, this group [a Living History class] brought out such beautiful memories, not always so beautiful, but still, all the pictures came up. It touched the layers of the kind that it was on those dead people already. It was laying on them like layers, separate layers of earth, and all of a sudden in this class I feel it coming up like lava . . . . It melted away . . . . And then . . . it looked like they were never dead. (Myerhoff, 1978, p. 39)

THE WHENS OF ACCOUNTS

While accounts are certainly formulated in a variety of circumstances in our lives, we believe that they are most crucial to people's adaptation at times of crisis or trauma. Such times compel attempts to understand and gain a sense of control. Accounts are often developed most fully after the problematic event is over or after its early impact, if its effects continue. As we suggest in chapter 3, the onset of a trauma may have such stunning impact that it renders account-making impossible. Then, we believe, an almost drive-like dynamic is operative until the act of account-making has occurred and been satisfied (see our further discussion of this "completion tendence" in chapter 3, p. 59–60). To return to our anonymously quoted opening epigraph, the general and figurative answer to "When do we develop accounts?" is when there is a "fall from perfection" or, in more psychological terms, when an event of such magnitude as to shake a person's reality or even self-identity occurs. More specifically, it has been reported that attributional activity (seeking causal explanations) occurs more often under negative than positive mood states (Schwarz and Clore, 1983) and for negative outcomes versus positive outcomes (Harvey and Smith, 1977).

THE WHO OF ACCOUNTS

Basically, our analysis of account-making suggests that anyone who grieves profoundly develops accounts. Thus far, no work has been done on possible personality correlates of account-making; clearly, such work may be productive. Given available evidence, it is now possible to say that women are both more active in their account-making than are men and the more adroit of the sexes in effectively expressing feelings in accounts. This type of evidence has been suggested by early work in the relationship literature using free-response measures of people's thoughts and feelings about conflict and separation (e.g., Weiss, 1975; Hill, Rubin, and Peplau, 1976; Orvis, Kelley, and Butler, 1976; Harvey, Wells, and Alvarez, 1978). More generally, these findings are consistent with the frequent observations that women are more articulate and expressive about their feelings or analyses of close relationships, or that they clearly think and feel about relationships to a greater degree than do men. We would caution that this apparent gender difference may be changing over time, as men are encouraged in their socialization to be more expressive and analytical about their close relationships.

Recent work on the application of attribution theory to marital distress suggests a somewhat more complex picture of men and women in distressed relationships. Holtzworth-Munroe and Jacobson (1985) report that, while women in distressed relationships engage in considerable attributional analysis throughout the relationship, men start to analyze in this way mainly when major problems begin to surface in the relationship. Holtzworth-Munroe and Jacobson conclude that men's attributional activities in such relationships may serve as a barometer of the status of the relationship; when they finally do begin to search for an understanding of what is wrong, it is probably too late.

THE HOWS OF ACCOUNTS

Accounts may be presented in several ways: they may be verbalized to others; or they may be written in the form of diaries or other personal records. Although there has been little formal work to substantiate this point, it would appear likely that accounts may be manifest in all forms of art and symbolic representation, from poetry and art to ancient Egyptian and other cultures' pictography and hieroglyphics.

Reporting accounts via conversation appears to be the most common "how." Such activity occurs most often in talk between close friends, lovers, and family members. But an interesting deviation from this pattern is people's tendency to report fragments of accounts to strangers in particular settings, such as the conversations that frequently develop between passengers on airplanes (Duck, 1988). Indeed, type of social setting appears to be an important determinant both of when and how accounts are reported, and of how personal relationships develop in general, and merits more attention by researchers in this field (Altman, 1989; Altman and Werner, 1985). The commonality of conversational accounting for the intimate details of one's life is illustrated in an advertisement in *Cosmopolitan* magazine. In this advertisement, entitled "Office Romance," the story of how new co-workers became involved while working together is told in a series of full-page photographs. The advertisement suggests that the woman involved enticed her new male acquaintance because of her very smart and diverse wardrobe (the clothes were the advertised products) and includes the following lines by the woman: "'We need a break.' My new teammate declared. 'Shall we continue our meeting over lunch?' Was I *about* to refuse?! We talked business for ten minutes, life histories for two hours. He's *not* married" (*Cosmopolitan*, July, 1989, p. 66).

Thus far, communication researchers, prominently including Giles, Williams, and Coupland (in press), are making the most rapid strides in discovering the role of talk and sociolinguistic factors in influencing close-relationship phenomena. But much more work on how people communicate accounts in their conversations with others is needed. We need to know, for example, if gender, age, and other demographic variables affect the process and how talk may reflect deeper psychological issues in the dyad and the individuals involved.

Another form in which accounts may occur, which to date has not received much attention, is that accounts may be developed and played out almost exclusively in one's own thoughts (for example, the obsessive review of an ended relationship in Weiss's (1975) work). A fragmentary type of account-making appears to be pervasive in the waking thoughts of many people. It may be compelled by nagging worries, unresolved mental turmoil, conflict about decisions to be made, or whatever; it is a frequent companion for most of us at one time or another. Intrapsychic account-making may also be occasioned by "mindless tasks", which induce one to daydream and develop stories of desired happenings in one's imagination. One of Myerhoff's (1978, p. 74) elderly interviewees suggests this latter condition for account-making: "If you cannot tell a story to yourself when you are sewing, you are lost anyway. The work has no beginning and no end, but the story is told, it goes on in the head."

Finally, some scholars of account-making emphasize its underlying knowledge structure (Burnett, McGhee, and Clarke, 1987). This knowledge structure, of which the individual may not be aware, is conceived to affect action and expectation. In such treatments, it is part of the account. As schematic knowledge structures, accounts are more like theoretical constructs than real stories and thoughts available to the account-maker. We shall treat the theoretical structure of accounts in more detail in chapter 3. It should be stressed here, however, that our own treatment of accounts will highlight their conscious, phenomenological character. While knowledge structures may reside in the submerged part of the account "iceberg," there is much about accounts that is readily available to self and others and that is operative in social interaction.

In short, accounts may be displayed or manifested in various ways, from written and spoken words, to private thoughts, to overt actions, including highly symbolic ones.

METHODOLOGY

How are accounts studied? Methodologically, the study of account-making can represent a relatively non-reactive type of investigation of various kinds of records or behavior (see Harvey, Turnquist, and Agostinelli, 1988). Going back to earlier work on attribution, it has been found that people will make unsolicited interpretive responses (Harvey et al., 1980). These qualitative responses are then (usually) coded into quantitative indices. The advantage of this approach is its non-reactivity (that is, respondents are not simply making attributions because they have been asked to do so).

Accounts have been studied using both quantitative and qualitative approaches. Qualitative approaches have evolved from several schools of thought, including dramatism, ethnomethodology, ethogeny, and social constructivism (see Gergen and Davis, 1985; Cochran, 1986). Masheter and Harris (1986) reported a case-study qualitative approach, which appears promising. In their technique, couples engaged in close relationships are asked to choose and reconstruct a scene complete with the lines of dialogue, which represents a recurring pattern in their relationship. Within each scene reported, the authors attempt to trace the participants' stories line by line, interpretation by interpretation, similar to the process of coding a video record.

In another approach, Baxter and Wilmot (1985) reported a study using an ethnographic interview to solicit informant accounts (in the same way as did Myerhoff, 1978). These accounts pertained to events in an opposite-sex relationship in which the informant was involved. Open-ended interviews were used to obtain the accounts. Then via a method of analytic induction (Bulmer, 1979), basic categories of taboo topics were developed from 172 overall topics. Bulmer's approach involves forming categories for taboo topics which in this study were based on a subsample of protocols deriving the interviews. The research revealed which topics were considered to be taboo in the relationships in question, and the informants' reasons for considering them so (see also Baxter, 1987).

Antaki (1989) has provided one of the most ambitious new approaches to the study of aspects of accounts and more generally to the investigation of structures of causal beliefs. Following Toulmin's (1958) Structure of Argument Method, Antaki's technique invites respondents to write causes for a controversial event on cards and then to arrange the cards so as to describe the interrelationships among the causes. The respondent then reproduces the pattern as a diagram, drawing arrows between causes and effects. Finally, the respondent defends each link made in the diagrammed network. Antaki has found that this approach produces different but highly systematic structures of beliefs and linkages depending upon the respondents' prior beliefs about the issue in question. Such an approach in a somewhat modified form might be of value in analysis of arguments presented by respondents in stories. Especially useful may be the idea of asking respondents to diagram interlocking links and to defend these proposed connections.

In the present authors' early work on accounts, we have treated accounts as an example of material containing both interpretative and non-interpretive (descriptive) material. As a set of reported thoughts and feelings, an account may contain constituent responses such as attributions of responsibility and blame, attributions of causality, trait evaluations of self and other, and so on. These attributions and other contextual features (for example, everything from more descriptive material to breaks in speech, rhetorical questions, exclamations, and the like) may be identified through coding of the material and may be expected to be sensitive indicators of account themes and conclusions.

Importantly, the investigator needs to try to obtain the contextual material because it may lead to different codings of the material. A sarcastically-stated positive trait ascription to one's partner, for instance, may not be coded as a positive attribution – other contextual information should be used to help with such subtleties of coding. Such an ascription might be: "You're such a perfect house-keeper." In the context of other information, this attribution may be coded as a criticism of other's housekeeping tendencies. As another example, short phrases as responses to probing interviews or survey questions may be qualitatively different from the free-form stories people tell. One of the methodological challenges of conducting research on accounts must be identifying some of the least common denominators of the account-making process. In constructing narratives, words and phrases may prove to be such basic components. We prefer to begin with the assumption that people's account-making may become manifest in a variety of forms, and that we can identify the connections between these manifestations as all part of the same process. This approach also is the parsimonious one: phrases are short stories, and stories are verbalized or written accounts. While these probing methods of account-making investigation present many problems, such as those of operational definition and coding, they also represent the likely technique of necessity for studying populations and issues about which we as scholars of the account-making process often care most (for example, populations who may be resistant to talking about personal traumas and difficulties that involve highly sensitive material).

More generally, scholars representing such diverse fields as cognitive sciences, archaeology, art history, ethnohistory, philosophy, and social anthropology are now engaged in considerable dialogue regarding how to use and interpret archival materials and artifacts in an attempt to understand human thought across different historical epochs. Our emphasis on the value of archival records reflecting account-making activity is consonant with this dialogue and suggests the need for more work on investigative techniques that may be specially designed to probe account-type records that are both contemporary and ages old.

As a final point, it has been contended that some types of research in the area of close relationships may in fact serve as a type of counseling for participants (Rubin and Mitchell, 1976). We endorse this position as it applies to the study of accounts as well. The interaction between investigator and research participants will be constructive to the extent that the investigator is careful in respecting participants' feelings and rights of privacy, and in handling the data. Perhaps a new topic for account-making researchers is that of the ethics of trying to obtain very privileged information about people's most heartfelt problems and their accounts about those problems. Overall in this book, we shall take the position that the telling of accounts, when done in the proper way and at the proper time, represents a key step in a healing process – maybe one of the most effective healing steps associated with great personal trauma.

SUMMARY

We have come some distance in this chapter in introducing the concepts of accounts and account-making, and giving them definition and characterization in social psychology and the social and behavioral sciences in general. We have noted that as formal concepts, these ideas are relatively new to the social and behavioral sciences, and that in psychology they have been primarily the offspring of work on attributional processes. We have focused on their whys, whens, whos, hows, and the methodology for studying accounts. In the next chapter, we shall review and discuss representative literature revealing a large body of concepts and theory that is highly relevant to our ideas about accounts. We end this first part of our story with a quote from Jean-Paul Sartre's autobiography. It is a quote that eloquently summarizes a theme of this book:

A man is always a teller of stories, he lives surrounded by his own stories and those of other people, he sees everything that happens to him *in terms* of these stories and he tries to live his life as if he were recounting it. (Sartre, 1964, p. 18)

2 Accounts and Account-making in Various Literatures

She knew the rules: if you slept with a man – not your husband – that was
adultery, and that was what she and William were negotiating. But this was
between her and William. William had some prior claim. She had loved him
before she had met Robert, and she believed that without William she might
not have known that any happiness could be hers. He had lifted some cloud
from around her, and she was grateful to him.

Laurie Colwin, Intimacy, in *The Lone Pilgrim*, 1981

A DIVERSITY OF RELEVANT WORKS

As the opening quotation to this chapter implies, we are rationaliz-
ing creatures. At the heart of much of the prior literature on
accounts is the idea that people regularly search for justifications for
their behavior. This chapter will provide a selective review of work
on accounts and account-making. The development of theory and an
empirical literature on accounts and account-making and related
ideas have been increasing rapidly during the last two decades. None
the less, as a formal scientific topic, these phenomena have received
only modest attention in the literature of psychology or other social
and behavioral sciences. That paucity, however, is misleading. A
much greater amount of relevant writing and research emerges when
we examine a broader literature, which is not necessarily scientific in
nature. Whether under the heading of work on story-telling, narratives, personal history, or other terms, there has been a plethora of

writing on these highly related topics in the last two decades. We believe that a general survey of these related ideas and topics will be instructive in locating the accounts topic in the literature. The literature we shall peruse is aimed both at specialized scholarly audiences and at the general public.

First, we shall note several relevant works to show how widely accounts and account-making are used as a centerpiece technique in writing for the general public. In each of these, the author uses the respondents' own accounts to illustrate ideas and promote arguments about the concept in question: Hunt's (1969) *The Affair: A Portrait of Extra-Marital Love in Contemporary America* provides a gripping analysis of extramarital relations at that historical point in the United States, and in so doing used people's accounts reflecting on their own extramarital affairs. Abramson's (1984) *Sarah: A Sexual Biography* reports on the sexual life and development of a young woman from college student to prostitute to middle-class wife and mother. Schuchter's (1986) *Dimensions of Grief* focuses on people's attempts to cope with the loss of loved ones. Rubin's (1983) *Intimate Strangers* analyzes men's and women's attempts to forge closeness in the midst of imposing dilemmas of changing times of values and identities. Vaughan's (1986) *Uncoupling* reports evidence on people's perceptions of the crucial turning-points in the failing of their close relationships. Matthew's (1986) *Friendships through the Life Course* focuses on people's life-long quest for personal friendships and transitions in them. Weissberg's (1985) *Children of the Night* concerns the causes and impacts of adolescent prostitution. Bernikow's (1987) *Alone in America* traces the plight of millions of Americans who experience major periods of loneliness in their lives. Lawson's (1988) *Adultery: An Analysis of Love and Betrayal* presents case-studies of adultery in marriage, and analyzes the psychological dynamics involved. Oliner and Oliner's (1988) *The Altruistic Personality* reports on characteristics of and accounts by persons who risked their lives to help Jews escape from the Nazis during World War II. Finally, accounts are a principal type of evidence presented by Lichtman and Taylor (1986) in their analysis of the close relationships of female cancer patients, and by Allen and Pickett (1987) in their interpretation of streams of action in the life-courses of women.

Other examples of the use of accounts by writers will be presented to demonstrate further their theorized role in people's search for meaning and purpose in their lives. In an analysis that is highly consistent with the theoretical model we present in chapter 3, Birren

(1987) has presented hypotheses about the merits of autobiographical writing. He suggests that when both young and old make their autobiographical statements, this step gives new meaning to their present lives by helping them understand their pasts more fully: "Writing an autobiography puts the contradictions, paradoxes and ambivalence of life into perspective. It restores our sense of self-sufficiency and personal identity that has been shaped by the crosscurrents and tides of life" (Birren, 1987, p. 91).

According to the prominent cognitive-perceptual psychologist Jerome Bruner (1987, 1989), aspects of culture that we often take for granted provide a fertile ground for studying how people assign meaning to their lives and present their lives as narrative. This emphasis on folk psychology, as Bruner calls it, is quite similar to other scholars' emphasis on the value of story-telling. Bruner suggests that when events are out of the ordinary, people construct stories around them. He indicates that our narratives need a disruption of the ordinary, much as we do when we see a figure against a ground, to help us explain the ultraordinary and heroic in ways that show events to be not independent of our wishes, likes, and dislikes – that this is not "a world of billiard balls" according to Bruner. He also notes that the ancient Greeks invented gods to explain the ultraordinary. (See the discussion in chapter 6 of evolutionary aspects of account-making, which involves the idea that account-making as we know it is a relatively recent event in the history of the human species.)

As an overall assumption in his focus on life as narrative, Bruner contends, "While the act of writing autobiography is new under the sun – like writing itself – the self-told life narrative is, by all accounts, ancient and universal. People anywhere can tell you some intelligible account of their lives" (1987, p. 16). Bruner advances a thesis that bears much similarity to our position in his argument that the self-telling of life-narratives may structure perceptual experience, organize memory, and segment and "purpose-build" the very events of our lives. He suggests that, in the end, we *become* the autobiographical narratives by which we "tell about" ourselves. Finally, consistent with a line of reasoning that we shall advance in the next chapter, Bruner suggests that the most important quality of pain to the individual is that it is a "mattering" human experience. The narrative or story helps make it matter.

The Pulitzer Prize-winning psychiatrist Robert Coles (1986, 1989) has also suggested the importance of story-telling as a vehicle for arriving at deeper and more telling meanings about life. He urges teachers to use story-telling (personal as well as literary master-pieces) to make education more inviting to students, and to teach ethics and morality in a way that is compelling. Coles (1989) describes his own medical education as having been enhanced when he took the advice of a senior doctor and listened to the stories told to him by patients. These were psychological stories, sustained personal stories concerning critical self-identity and other important health-relevant information. Coles suggests that the story-telling was conducive to better diagnostic work and, moreover, contributed to the patients' ultimate health. He concludes his commentary on the development of story-telling as part of his learning experience with this perceptive remark about the overarching meaningfulness of the narrative: "Such a respect for narrative as everyone's rock-bottom capacity, but also as the universal gift, to be shared with others, seemed altogether fitting" (1989, p. 30).

Similar types of quest to find meaning are posited in the powerful and classic works by Frankl (1963) and Klinger (1977) in their treatments of how people try to deal with difficulties that involve despair and feelings of meaninglessness and anomie in their lives. Klinger's influential book, *Meaning and Void*, advances what he calls incentive theory to explain why people pursue so many different avenues in their drive to make their lives more meaningful. But it was Frankl who first and most convincingly argued that a sense of meaning is centrally important in a person's life, not as a philosophical abstraction but as a potential life-or-death factor in human survival. According to Frankl, meaning consists of searching for a purpose or task with which to define one's life. He illustrates well the quinti-essential search for meaning in describing his own efforts to survive a Nazi concentration camp. These efforts involved writing a book-length manuscript by surreptitiously working on fragments of toilet paper. The manuscript was later discovered and destroyed by a guard, but it was retained in part in Frankl's memory and became the basis for his work *Man's Search for Meaning*.

These works illustrate the vast literature of writing and research that has involved the use of accounts to explore humans' grappling with many types of dilemma. Such works delve deeply into issues and have wide popular appeal because they emphasize the ordinary, common-sense reports of individuals experiencing problems. They also take advantage of people's common need and quest to share their stories with interested others.

REVIEW OF RELEVANT SCHOLARLY LITERATURE

Accounts may be viewed as a broad concept bearing considerable similarity to other concepts in the social and behavioral sciences literature. Defined as packages of interpretations and expressions occurring in story form, account-like conceptions have an extensive history. They are similar to the classic concepts of "vocabularies of motive" postulated by C. Wright Mills (1940) and the "grammar of motives" proposed by Burke (1945). According to Mills, popular beliefs concerning what constitutes adequate grounds for various acts differ across groups and cultures. In each group, people's actions are classified somewhat differently, and there are common understandings concerning the plausible reason for each category of action. This notion suggests that there is a distinct vocabularly of motives in each discrete cultural group. For example, in the 1980s in the United States, hedonistic, materialistic ("get-ahead") motives for action on the part of young, ambitious, professionals have been fashionable. Such "motives" may well prove less popular as we enter the 1990s. What will be interesting to assess over time is whether people's accounts also reflect sociological (as well as linguistic) features. Mills' formulation stressed the importance of the use of *motive talk* to ward off or revise potential or actual questioning of the motives underlying action.

Burke's concept of grammars of motives is quite similar to Mills' ideas and our own view of accounts in that it refers to words, phases, and clauses that people use to justify action (for example, I hit her because she always nagged me). In this sense, accounts often subsume several different grammars of motives. Burke emphasized the persuasive aspect of such grammars, quite apart from their plausibility regarding the real bases for an action. As Simons (1989) notes, Burke "is simply less interested in causes *per se* than in the accounts people provide of causation. Even during his most strongly Marxist period he recognized that material conditions of existence do not achieve their full social significance until they are *inscribed in accounts*" (our emphasis). In this respect Burke bears strong affinity with ethnomethodologists and with attribution theorists in psychology. In *A Grammar of Motives*, Burke takes special delight in laying bare the rhetoric of accounts; that is, the ways they exploit the "resources of ambiguity" in language (1945, p. 13; quoted in Simons and Melia (eds), 1989, a volume that contains useful reviews and analyses of Burke's thinking). This idea of ambiguity attending language and hence accounts is similar to the argument by the attribution theorists Snyder and Wicklund (1981), who suggest that people often prefer the ambiguity surrounding causality in social life; given such ambiguity, Snyder and Wicklund suggest, attributors can more readily make inferences that enhance their sense of control.

The direction of viewing account-making as persuasion deserves further research in the accounts and attribution research traditions, and has been given some attention by Orivs, Kelley and Butler (1976) and Newman (1981) who have emphasized the persuasive nature of many attributions people make to their partners in close relationships. In chapter 8, we shall discuss how account-making as persuasion may represent a useful direction for further research.

More generally, accounts may be viewed as related to Osgood's (1962) emphasis on judgement. He argued that many cultures and societies use judgement to order experience and to facilitate understanding of human action. Judgement, in this approach, involves comparison of experience against some abstract dimension or against one's imagination. Often central to account-making is such a judgemental process. Osgood suggests that across cultures, people regularly engage in a meaning search involving judgemental activities (see Maddi, 1970, for a further discussion of this evaluation process). His reasoning may be compared to the explicit accounts conception of Semin and Manstead (1983; see pp. 31–2 below), who contend that all judgements pertaining to social actions are evaluative or have evaluative implications. This evaluative context presumably sets the stage for the continual need on the part of the individual to account for any type of act that may be questioned by others.

FIRST EXPLICIT TREATMENTS

The accounts concept was first explicitly advanced by a cadre of sociologists over two decades ago. The writings of Goffman (1959, 1971), Garfinkel (1956, 1967), and Scott and Lyman (1968; Lyman and Scott, 1970) were at the forefront of this theoretical development. Goffman's (1959) seminal work on self-presentation, *The Presentation of Self in Everyday Life*, represents the conceptual foundation for many contemporary theories and empirical research programs regarding how people tactically present themselves to others. This includes work on account-making. Goffman (1971) contended that when a person commits an offense, a powerful societal script for account-making is set in motion, to wit: a demand is placed on the offender to provide an account in order to nullify the negative implications concerning the offender's regard for the identity of the offended party or parties. Such a script is part of the embedded routine of social interaction. Offenses must be explained in order for an interrupted flow of interaction to resume.

In the context of the "Red Scare" in the United States and Senator McCarthy's purges in the 1950s, Garfinkel (1956) wrote eloquently about how people's personal worth may be degraded in societal and institutional rituals. Garfinkel (1967) also analyzed the activities whereby members of society organize and manage everyday affairs and, in the process, make actions accountable. He suggested that accountability may be taken for granted in such affairs, becoming more salient when the circumstances become problematic. He emphasized that actions are organized in such a way that they can be accountable for to others and that that accountability of actions is a pervasive part of human life.

It was Scott and Lyman's writings that were most explicit in delineating account strategies in various types of social situation and that had the most direct impact on later work on account-making research. The background for Scott and Lyman's theoretical work appears to be varied. As Schoenbach (1980) suggests, they were influenced by Sykes and Matza's (1957) analysis of techniques of neutralization and justification which delinquents learn as facilitators and minimizers of deviant acts. But their theory is also applicable to non-criminal, failure events. Failure events refer both to deviant acts committed and obligations omitted. Scott and Lyman defined the account as "a linguistic device employed whenever an action is subjected to valuative inquiry" (Scott and Lyman, 1968, p. 46). Thus, at the outset of this discussion, the reader should note the narrow way Scott and Lyman define an account compared to the way we have defined an account.

Scott and Lyman argued that there are two general types of accounts: justifications or excuses about socially undesirable actions. It may be inferred from their analysis that the motivation for such accounts is protection of self-esteem or social status. Excuses, which in this conception are statements used to relieve the actor of responsibility, are conceived as occurring in the modal forms of appeal to accidents, defeasibility, biological drives, and scapegoating. An example of scapegoating they give is the following statement, made by a woman: "I was always getting into fights because some girls are vipers; they get jealous, tell lies about each other and start trouble" (Scott and Lyman, 1968, p. 50). Similarly, Scott and Lyman contended that justifications are socially approved vocabularies that neutralize an act or its consequences. They noted four types of justification: denial of injury, denial of victim (that is, that the victim deserved the harm), appeal to loyalties (that is, that the actor was acting in the interests of the victim), and condemnation of condemners. An example of a justificatory account (in the form of an appeal to loyalties) is the following statement by a mentally ill patient: "I was going to night school to get an M.A. degree, and holding down a job in addition, and the load got too much for me" (Scott and Lyman, 1968, p. 52).

VARIED STRANDS OF RELATED WORK IN 1970s AND 1980s

The value of the early work on accounts, in particular Scott and Lyman's writings, has only fully been recognized in the last decade. Interestingly, this recognition did not occur in their field of sociology to any appreciable degree. Rather, it has occurred among communication scholars, social psychologists, and, in particular, close-relationship researchers. Three early follow-up refinements on Scott and Lyman's position are: Prus's (1975) discussion of the many tactics of resistance that people may use against attributions of responsibility for a failure event; a subdivision of justifications by Harré (1977), which distinguished between the intelligibility and the warrantability of actions and discussed corresponding strategies of accounting; and Blumstein et al.'s (1974) experimental study, which evaluated conditions under which people will respect others' accounts (for example, moral worth, as by a show of penitence, and the offender's personal control over the offense were found to be major determinants). We shall next review related work emerging from the communication and social psychology literatures.

Scott and Lyman's treatment emphasized accounts as given in talk. A more recent treatment, which focuses on talk and analyzes excuses and justifications offered by people in various social settings, is provided by Semin and Manstead (1983). These scholars were concerned primarily with the accountability of conduct. By this they mean that people are held to be responsbile for their actions. When these actions are thought to be questionable (involving, as they term it, "fractured social interaction"), the individual concerned feels obliged by others to provide an account. In this framework, actions that correspond to social expectations are not called into question and hence do not lead to account-making. Semin and Manstead define an account as "an explanation of the actions that mitigates either the actor's responsibility for the action or the questionability of the action" (Semin and Manstead, 1983, p. x): "The medium for these accounting practices is *talk*, and talk therefore constitutes the central object of our inquiry." Semin and Manstead argue that the communicative processes involved in the accountability of conduct consist of interpretations which unfold as part of the ongoing negotiations of meanings between participants (in fact, the believe that the general attribution approach has so many limitations that they have decided to refer to their approach instead as "interpretative social psychology").

Much theoretical and empirical work in social psychology has relied on ideas that, while consistent with the account-making logic outlined above, did not explicitly focus on accounts. Jellison's (1977) provocative analysis of how people use lies to present themselves so as to protect their self-interests and maximize personal rewards is illustrative. Like Scott and Lyman, Jellison stressed social justification as the key motivation for the presentation of account-like material. But he did not present an analysis of account-making or the contents of accounts. He did argue that self-justifying presentations are designed to win approval from others and that their content is influenced by this motivation. If the individual achieves such support from others, he or she is more likely to gain material resources from them. In this vein, Snyder, Higgins, and Stucky (1983) suggest that people employ various excuses to maintain self-esteem. These include "retrospective" excuses which are most relevant to accounts. A retrospective excuse involves reconstructing the past to make oneself appear more appealing. (See Weber, Harvey and Stanley, 1987, for a fuller discussion of this inviting line of work.)

Another form of excuse-making having relevance to brief accounting is providing excuses for rejecting overtures for social engagements. Folkes (1982) has provided interesting data on the typical excuses college students make for rejecting date offers, showing people's tendency to avoid attributions to others' personal qualities and to emphasize situational problems, such as need to study for an important exam. Similarly, Metts (1989) explored students' free-response descriptions of situations involving deception of a close-relationship partner. She also found evidence of protective strategies especially among married individuals, who indicated that they had used deception on occasion in order to avoid threats to their spouse's self-esteem.

The focus on social justification is also related to the social-resource exchange literature of factors involved in viewing others accountable (or negotiating with others about accountability) in exchange situations (Couch and Weiland, 1986). Again, the emphasis is not so much on the content of the "holding of other accountable," or the impact thereof, as it is on the conditions under which one may be held accountable. Relatedly, Tetlock and colleagues (e.g. Tetlock and Boettger, 1989) have conducted an interesting strand of research which emphasizes the differential cognitive and judgemental effects of whether or not people feel that they are publicly accountable for their actions.

Another fascinating program of work on accountability is being implemented by Schlenker and colleagues (Schlenker and Weigold, in press; Schlenker, Weigold, and Doherty, in press). These scholars argue that self-identification can be regarded as accounting and that people regularly employ strategies of presentation, including self-serving accounts, in order to validate desired identity images (see also discussion of the self in chapter 8).

A recent program of work in the area of communication research is directly linked to Lyman and Scott's seminal analysis. Cody, McLaughlin, and colleagues' work stands out as a systematic pursuit of the types of justification people give for failure events or social predicaments. An interesting illustration of their work is found in McLaughlin, Cody, and O'Hair's (1983) investigations of retrospective reports of reproaches given by a sample of college students. One such reproach was: "My husband said, 'Where the hell have you been? Did you forget to wind your watch again?'" McLaughlin et al. describe this reproach as a projected excuse; that is, the questioner offers it as a possible justification to the person who must answer for some problematic behavior. As Cody and McLaughlin (in press, p. 4) describe the domain of their work: "We emphasize . . . studies on 'communicated' explanations; that is, communication episodes in which an accounter offers an apology, excuse, justification, or denial to a parent or other family member, friend, lover, traffic officer, parole officer, judge, jury, etc." Other important work in this area includes Schoenbach (1980), who theorized that the account sequence involves a failure event, a reproach, an account, and an evaluation. Schoenbach also provided an elaborate extension and refinement of Scott and Lyman's taxonomy for account phrases.

It is not always clear in the foregoing strands of work whether the account-maker is aware that he or she is engaging in strategic justification. However, Goffman (1959), and a compelling analysis by Greenwald (1980), suggest that, on many occasions, people are highly aware of their tactical activity. Greenwald suggests that people readily revise and fabricate personal history in the service of self-esteem and self-interest. Also, as will be discussed in chapter 6, it appears that people may engage in strategic planning, which then structures account-making and related behavior (Berger, 1988).

Regarding these researchers' focus on social predicaments and related situations, we agree that such a focus covers many of the situations in which accounts may be given. But it does not subsume those involving highly positive effects, or events in which the individual may reasonably be seen as a victim (events that are negative in consequence for the actor but in which the actor need not try to justify his or her causal role – see later discussion of victimization research, p. 41). There is another important point from our perspective to make about the foregoing work on accounts for social predicaments and excuse-making in general. We would contend that the brief phrase often studied as the primary response in these investigations suggests but does not provide the "whole story" surrounding the event in question. For example, the reproach studied by McLaughlin et al., in which the husband asked his wife where she had been, may suggest a more complete story of marital conflict, the husband's suspicion about the wife's infidelity, and generally a negative cycle of accusation, blame, and excuse-making. Whatever the reproach–justification sequence implies, it probably relates to a fuller story about the relationship. It is this fuller story which our approach seeks to understand. At the same time, we commend those scholars who are systematizing our understanding of the portion of the story that involves justification and excuse-making, and the nature and conditions for these responses.

A conception of accounts that is quite similar to our own position is articulated by Antaki (1987). He describes various types of accounts within close relationships, emphasizing their function, and in so doing he makes a perceptive distinction between performable accounts (these a person could display to others) and unperformable accounts. These latter accounts, which we believe form part of the body of our accounts repertoires, exist quietly and are not readily displayable (perhaps because they contain potentially embarrassing material). None the less, Antaki contends that such unperformable accounts may be effective in determining a person's actions, thoughts, and feelings. We have suggested in chapter 1 that the private version of accounts essentially may be a "master account" (or life-story) requiring many years to develop, and requiring much of one's life in order for its fullness to be a matter of conscious reflection for the account-maker. In general, we believe that Antaki's distinction speaks to the hidden issues in the nature of accounts such as when they will be performable vs. unperformable, to whom they will be performable, why they will become performable, how much strategy goes into the decision to perform and actual performance, and the consequences of performance vs. non-performance. Antaki's provocative reasoning needs to be tied more closely to the work discussed earlier on justifications and excuse-making. Scholars focusing on accounts as justifications and excuses may not be giving enough attention to these nuances of performance.

In addition to the literature outlined above, the notions of accounts and account-making have been presented as they relate to people's feelings of jealousy. Van Sommers (1988) argues that people often refer to their close relationships in terms of their investments, which may include possessions, time and energy, and even children; and believe that they should be able to take out of a relationship at least what they put into it. Van Sommers calls this type of thinking "practical accounting." It undoubtedly involves story-telling, justification, and many of the other elements of accounts and account-making that we have discussed above. More generally, van Sommers asserts that jealous lovers use a variety of tests and tricks to try to "find out" the improprieties of their partners. It is suggested that such tactics are premised on the stories of their partners – stories that are believed to involve lying. Here are some of van Sommers' respondents' examples of accounts that had led to such suspicion.

> Larry always wore striped ties. His wife had fallen into the habit of noting the direction of the stripe in his tie in the mornings. She realized his tie had been retied during the day.

> Paul bought a very trendy overcoat with a hood. His wife's 'immediate instinct' was that 'he'd got it bad for a very young girl'.

> Mark and his wife used to read the astrology charts together. She saw him read a new sign, smile, and say nothing.

> Victor became a Beethoven fanatic. His wife guessed the other woman was a music lover. (1988, p. 179)

Our Position

It should be clear from the discussion of these related positions that we view accounts in much broader terms than earlier theorists. In addition to social justification, we have noted as bases for account-making the enhancement of a personal sense of control and closure, catharsis and emotional release, sheer desire to understand, and quest to achieve enlightened feeling and enhanced will and hope.

Thus, we argue that accounts should be treated as a broad, heurstic concept. We also believe that accounts may occur in a variety of formats in addition to that of verbal statements, as was suggested by Lyman and Scott, Semin and Manstead, and others. Finally, we have construed account-making as a much broader type of enterprise than is theorized in these other models. In contrast to these other positions, we emphasize both the process of account-making and the contents of this process. Further, we believe that account-making is a near-continuous process, if only implicitly, and that it may be initiated for any type of action, including "fractured social interaction," smooth, facilitative interaction, and private behavior.

ACCOUNTING FOR RELATIONSHIPS

In 1987, Burnett, McGhee and Clarke edited and published the first volume of collected writings on account-making in close relationships. This volume reflects many of the themes discussed above, as well as a diversity of conceptions of accounts. The volume's contributors also point to many directions for further inquiry. The editors themselves pose several important questions, including: How reflective are people in relationships (Burnett, 1987); if they typically are not reflective, do they mainly move into account-making phases when problems emerge? How important are actual, practical, linguistic aspects of the situation in which accounts are given to the content and consequences of account-making (McGhee, 1987)? Do speakers sometimes create accounts on the spot, as it were, to justify earlier claims, and do they then sometimes persuade themselves about the merit/veracity of their own accounts (McGhee, 1987)? Our response at this stage to these questions is, first, as we suggest repeatedly in the present book, people may do more implicit account-making than explicit account-making; and second, indeed, there is a great need for work on the sociolinguistic aspects of account-making as well as their self- and other-persuasion effects. Giles and colleagues (e.g. Giles, Williams, and Coupland, in press) eloquently suggest such a need in the general domain of work on communication.

A final important direction for accounts research signaled in the Burnett et al. (1987) volume concerned methodology. Duck (1987) argued persuasively that this area of work should direct its prime focus on process variables and longer-term relationships between real people. More generally, Duck and colleagues have provided cogent analyses of the value of process analysis (emphasizing the "how" and "why" of relationship development) in the study of personal relationships (Duck and Sants, 1983; Duck, 1988).

COMPARISON WITH WORK ON NARRATIVES

In our own work (e.g. Harvey, Orbuch, and Weber, 1990), we have suggested that there is considerable similarity between theory and research on accounts and theory and research on narratives. The standard definition of narrative connotes an individual telling his or her story, usually orally. To the extent that the concept of narrative may be broadened to encompass other forms of expression and even mental representation, we do not believe that the ideas of account and narrative need to be differentiated in any formal sense. There is a useful literature emerging on narratives that contributes to our present understanding of accounts and account-making (e.g. Mancuso and Sarbin, 1983; Gergen and Gergen, 1984, 1987, 1988; Cochran, 1986; Cochran and Claspell, 1987). The Gergens' writing, in particular, has been helpful in postulating narrative structures, or story-forms within different social milieux and cultures. Gergen and Gergen (1987) suggest that the well-formed narrative possesses these components: (1) the establishment of a goal state (e.g. an end-point of the story, such as "how I escaped death"); (2) selection of events relevant to the goal state (e.g. the relevant acts regarding "my escape"); (3) arrangement of events in chronological order; (4) establishing causal linkages (e.g. "My escape, therefore, was due mostly to my own courage"); and (5) demarcation signs (e.g. openings such as "Have you heard this one?", and concluders such as "So now you know what happened"). The value of order in narrative sequences is emphasized by Arntson and Droge (1987) in a study of the communication dynamics found in epilepsy self-help groups. They suggest that narrative order ("A happened, then B") makes the events portrayed seem more understandable and the future more predictable for the narrator.

Gergen and Gergen (1987) also suggest that people, in effect, use self-presentation tactics in telling their stories, which often have strongly positive or negative themes. If a couple in a close relationship state that they are experiencing frequent "highs" and "lows" in their "relationship story", the Gergens imply that the couple would be showing the story-form of a romantic saga (which, we would add, is a common story-form for many long-term close relationships). The Gergens argue that stories are frequently changed by actors in accordance with circumstance. They state, "The emerging love story may be abandoned when a worthy competitor arrives to make his/her bid for intimacy" (1987, p. 285). The Gergens' analysis is especially engaging regarding the nature and dynamics of close-relationship narratives. However, as for their general argument, we would counter that account-making does not always involve telling one's story to another in a narrative format. Account-making, likewise may be done in writing (e.g. diaries) or in private mental reflections, and it may be more fragmented and chaotic than the coherent patterning suggested by the Gergens for narratives.

In a more recent statement, Gergen and Gergen (1988) contend that furnishing an account is a behavior in the present that is a response to current circumstances. They reject the view that people carry with them fully elaborated narratives of all events that can be presented upon demand. We agree in part with this reasoning. Certainly, the act of presenting an account may by itself affect the contents of the presentation (see also discussion in chapter 8). Further, we find congenial an implication of the Gergens' (1988) argument that narratives of the same event may change over time and presentation. However, we do not believe that accounts, especially those of compelling life-events, are so flimsily lodged in our psyches, as the Gergens' analysis might suggest. Rather, the themes and some of the lines for crucial stories seem indelibly grafted into our memories (e.g. a man's account theme of why his wife left him). Whether or not such themes and lines are presented when a person feels stimulated to provide a narrative to an other may be determined by many factors, including the circumstances surrounding the request and imputed caring and empathy to other.

One other analysis of narratives merits analysis in connection with our discussion of accounts. Shotter (1984, 1987) has made valuable contributions to the literature on narratives and accounts. One general idea that derives from his analysis is that accounts or narratives are always constructed and are contextualized within larger explanatory systems (all-embracing accounts for particular events; e.g. a lover's overall account for his or her love-life, which subsumes and helps explain any particular love relationship). On the importance of the narrative Shotter says: "In my view it works *retrospectively*, to make some sense of what has happened so far, to gain hints as to what might happen next" (1987, p. 233).

In his analysis of accounts, Shotter (1984) has focused on how people talk about themselves and their behavior and, in general, make their conduct accountable in a moral world. One difference with our position, though, is that Shotter follows the rule-oriented view of ethogenic psychology (see discussion below, p. 42) in emphasizing how people *must talk* about themselves in terms of the social order and socially constructed morality in which they exist. People, thus, must account for their experiences in ways that are intelligible and legitimate in their current social context. Our analysis is less formal in this regard, but also involves the view that account-making occurs in a social context and may be affected in substantive ways by this context. We also believe that there may be more flexibility in the social order for different types of account-making, or talking about accounts, than is implied in Shotter's analysis.

MAINSTREAM ATTRIBUTION WORK

As described in chapter 1, psychological social psychologists concerned with the application of attributional theoretical ideas to understanding close relationships (e.g. Harvey, Wells, and Alvarez, 1978) were among the first scholars to pursue the accounts topic in social psychology. This work was stimulated by Weiss's (1975) persuasive use of the concept in his study of marital separation. At that point, these attribution scholars focused in large part on the methodological advantage of permitting respondents to engage in more elaborate responses. Accounts and account-making, at that time, were not reated as having major interest and theorectical value in and of themselves. Essentially, accounts were seen as packages of attributions (including attributions of causality, responsibility, and blame, and trait ascriptions both to other and self) and descriptive material. In related attribution research, progress was made in developing techniques to measure attributions as free responses, or as relatively unsolicited activity (Harvey et al., 1980; Wong and Weiner, 1981). A timely and searching analysis of this early work in the context of the development of attribution approaches is provided by Hewstone (1989).

Only in the 1980s did attribution scholars begin to formulate explicit accounts-oriented theories and link their work to the earlier work such as that by Lyman and Scott and to the then emerging prolific strand of work on accounts in Great Britain. Further, in the late 1970s, these attribution workers began to appreciate more fully the value of examining attributions *within the context of natural stories* that people tell about their lives. This interest resulted in

Harvey and Weber's (1982) presentation, on an attributional analysis of termination of close relationships with a special focus on the account, at the first International Conference on Personal Relationships (see Harvey et al., 1986). Thus, historically, accounts work has its genesis in attribution theory and research in social psychology.

More recently, Read (1987) has provided an interesting knowledge-structure approach to causal reasoning that emphasizes people's roles as storytellers and story-understanders. In these roles, Read argues that people take sequences of actions and integrate them into a coherent, plausible scenario. People presumably do so via the drawing of numerous inferences based on detailed knowledge about people and the world. Also, in a series of valuable studies, Huston, Cate, Surra, and their colleagues have used account-like probes to examine how couples explain the decision-making processes involved in their movement toward or away from marriage (e.g. Huston et al., 1981; Surra, 1985).

As Read has suggested, this storyteller narrative-knower approach is consistent with Heider's (1958) statement on the dynamics of social perception, which emphasized the merit of studying people's naive causal theories. Similarly, in the area of social perception, cognitive psychologists concerned with story schemata and scripts (e.g. J. M. Mandler, 1984) often work on problems quite distant from the nature of people's account-making activities. Nevertheless, we shall probably find a fertile interface awaiting the scholar who can readily make connections between these disparate literatures on account-making regarding molar social events and schema activity in recall and recognition phenomena. We believe that accounts, like schemata, affect future encoding of information, anticipation and reconstruction of events, and social interaction patterns.

Coming out of the attribution tradition, Thompson and Janigian (1988) have presented a useful analysis that is relevant to our treatment of accounts. They suggest that life schemata may provide a framework for understanding people's search for meaning. They state that a life schema is like a story with oneself as the protagonist. In their approach, a story has four basis elements: (1) a protagonist – a central character seen from the author's perspective; (2) a plot – problems to be overcome and goals that the protagonist wishes to attain; (3) events that are relevant to these problems or goals; and (4) a world-view – the author's, usually unstated, assumptions about how life operates (e.g. "People get what they deserve", "God puts obstacles in your path to help you grow"). One's own life schema involves each of these elements and their constituents. For example, for the protagonist, one has a sense of personal ability and resources, feelings of personal control, and so on. Thompson and Janigian (1988) suggest that this concept of life schema integrates the two sides of meaningfulness – order provided by a stable world and self-view, and purpose provided by goals and some likelihood they can be attained.

A final strand of work within the attribution literature that has relevance to accounts concerns people's perceptions of themselves as victims or the significant others of victims. The questions of interest have focused on attributions about the causes of a major harmful event in the life of the victim. An emerging literature on this topic reveals, for example, that victims of negative life-events often experience loss of meaning, a need for discussion of the event with others, and persistent, intrusive ruminations concerning the event (Tait and Silver, 1989). Although not all victims experience this set of severely debilitating symptoms, most victims experience some adjustment difficulties, and it is likely that some facet of account-making is central to their attempts to cope with the problem. Notable work on the particular kinds of attribution (usually not presented in story-form) made by victims and the causal status of those attributions is reported and/or analyzed by Janoff-Bulman and Wortman (1977), Janoff-Bulman and Frieze (1983), Taylor, Wood, and Lichtman (1983), and Turnquist, Harvey, and Andersen (1988). Another fascinating line of research in this area has focused on people's reactions to victims (see also chapter 4) for related work on accounts and person perception. Lerner (1980) hypothesizes that people believe victims deserve what they get in life and get what they deserve. Lerner has developed and tested this hypothesis within the context of his just world theory which suggests that people believe that pain and loss are not inflicted on others in a random manner; rather they believe that the world is just and that a victim's losses are deserved. (The reader is referred to Weary, Stanley, and Harvey (1989) for a recent review of much of this research.)

It should be noted that, increasingly, research in the area of victimization is examining accounts as part of the victims' responses, although so far the concepts of accounts or account-making have not been widely and explicitly recognized as having importance in the victimization process. In chapter 3, we shall outline a theoretical model that begins to speak to the merit of considering this process and consequent coping behavior.

THE ETHOGENIC POSITION ON ACCOUNTS

Harré and colleagues (e.g. Harré and Secord, 1972; Harré, 1979) have written a number of influential treatises outlining what they call "ethogenic psychology." In this approach, Harré and colleagues seek to explain social behavior, emphasizing non-mechanistic models. They assume that both the production of skilled and competent action and the ability to provide accounts are grounded in a culturally provided pool of knowledge. This view has been challenged by other theorists. For example, Semin and Manstead (1983) argue that tacit knowledge may play a prominent role in account-making, and that on occasion people may employ extemporaneously derived accounts in deference to the culturally-furnished possible explanations. Harré and associates have focused explicitly on accounts data in some of their writings to make relevant arguments.

Harré, Clark, and DeCarlo (1985), for example, assert that in producing their accounts, actors are displaying knowledge of the ideal ways of acting and ideal reasons for doing what they have done or omitted doing. These authors state "When we collect the accounts from a subculture, like football fans, or a family, or a hospital ward, etc., we search through the accounts for descriptions of what *should* happen. And we *represent* this material as a system of rules *representing a system of knowledge and beliefs*" (Harré et al., 1985, p. 88). They go on to say that the rules so cited can be checked against the ethnographic hypotheses about the meanings of the actions, and these accounts are not introspective descriptions of cognitive processes such as plans and intentions.

We have no qualms with this rule-oriented conception in depicting the underlying structure of account-making. We do, however, accord significance to the original contents of the reported knowledge displayed by actors, whether or not this knowledge always reflects ideal ways of acting and reasons for action. We also value such contents even if they do not seem to cohere with the most scientifically plausible explanations for the event in question. The original contents (including reports of plans and intentions), style of presentation, and context of the report are of primary importance to our analysis. In defense of these scholars who argue from the ethogenic position, the accounts topic appears to be of secondary importance in their array of central ideas about how social behavior should be studied.

SUMMARY

We have seen that the literature pertinent to accounts and account-making derives from many sources. In this chapter, we first noted examples of the uses of accounts and account-making as a case-making approach to the study of many societal issues in the general literature. We reviewed a wide literature explicitly on accounts, beginning with early work by a group of sociologists. We also reviewed many ideas and strands of work that we consider relevant to the accounts topic. Certainly, it is true that many of these concepts and lines of research are linked only indirectly to our topic. However, even among indirect relatives, the links to the central story-like and story-telling aspects of accounts and account-making are unmistakable. We could also sample the great literatures of the world and find many other related ideas.

Overall, we have attempted to establish the psychological value and relevance of accounts and account-making. We believe that these concepts deserve a place in the spectrum of useful theoretical ideas in contemporary psychology and in related behavioral sciences. In the next chapter, we shall present our own theoretical model of the account-making process in response to severe stress. As we end this review chapter, we hope that the reader agrees with our argument that a more compelling social psychology of account-making will emphasize the breadth of the account and its rich implications for the way we live our lives. Jerome Bruner arrived at a somewhat similar conclusion in his relatively new pursuit of the topic of life as narrative: "I cannot imagine a more important psychological research project than one that addresses itself to the 'development of autobiography' – how our way of telling about ourselves changes, and how these accounts come to take control of our ways of life. Yet I know of not a single comprehensive study on this topic" (Bruner, 1987, p. 15).

3 A Theoretical Conception of Account-making in Response to Severe Stress

> Give sorrow words: the grief that does not speak
> Whispers the o'er-fraught heart, and bids it break.

Shakespeare, Macbeth

INTRODUCTORY COMMENTS

As the great playwright and "psychologist of his time" Shakespeare suggests, the act of speaking about grief may serve to ease that grief. The purpose of this chapter is to present a theoretical conception of the possible role of account-making in response to severe stress. We suggested in chapter 1 that no one who lives long enough is immune to the psychological and physical tolls exacted by significant stressors. Whether experiencing divorce, backruptcy, being fired, the loss of a close colleague, or knowledge that one's spouse has a terminal illness, such events punctuate and sometimes pervade the course of every human life. Vast numbers of people are seeking solutions for how to deal with their personal crises. They are looking to self-help groups, books or therapists, the media (with the currently ubiquitous television talk-show speaking to some of this need for a forum in which to vent; see Carbaugh, 1988). In this context, there has been a tidal wave of writing and media work devoted to people telling their stories of how they coped or are coping with traumatic circumstances. Examples of this type of presentation include Morrell's (1988) *Fireflies* (described in chapter

1), and a 1988 television special on breast cancer entitled "Destined to Live: 100 Roads to Recovery", in which a number of well-known women including the actresses Jill Eikenberry and Jill Ireland discussed their fight against breast cancer.

We live in a time of widespread emotional vulnerability and concomitant susceptibility to all types of healing agents and approaches. In the United States since 1986, "Baby Boomers" – those born shortly after World War II – have been moving into their forties at the rate of four million a year. This generation has known both prosperity and stress in large measure, and is most responsible for the epidemic of so-called "mid-life crises", which affect so many individuals and their families. For young and old alike, the last quarter of the century has involved much cultural flux. There has been an increase in homelessness throughout the world. There has been a revival of cults and Satanic-ritual focused groups in the USA, one of which was responsible for the killing and dismemberment of an American college student in Matamoros, Mexico, in 1989. A never-ending stream of charismatic father-figures has emerged to lead people seeking assurance and direction, including the Reverend Jim Jones of Jonestown notoriety, and a host of television evangelists, each claiming to tell us the way to salvation and how to address both the banal and sublime dilemmas of living – as well as how to spend our money. These cultural developments have many origins, including prominently a disarray in societal mechanisms that traditionally have served to enhance coping, such as the nuclear family and the Church. Such mechanisms appear to be breaking down, often under the weight of people's problems, or collapsing in inefficiency.

Within this context of cultural flux, one theme of this book is that greater educational emphasis upon systematic, in-depth account-making may prove to be one of the most promising approaches to coping with life's major stresses. The ability to try to account for one's problems or the problematic events one observes is, as Coles (1989) notes, everyone's universal gift or capacity of last resort. We believe that the public at large, as well as the enormous and proliferating health-service provider community, needs to be much more familiar with this logic and to work toward preserving and nourishing the universal gift of account-making.

In this chapter we shall present a general commentary on severe stress as a research topic, a recent model of account-making under conditions of severe stress (Harvey, Orbuch, and Weber, 1990), and a related analysis of social-psychological processes associated with account-making. A central proposition of this chapter is that accounts matter; they empower our will and impassion our senses; they affect our thoughts, feelings, and actions, and may just as readily be treated as independent as well as dependent variables in research studies.

THE NATURE OF SEVERE STRESS AND ITS STUDY

Traumatic-stress studies encompass the investigation of the immediate and long-term psychosocial consequences of highly stressful events and the factors that affect those consequences. As an emerging hybrid field involving researchers from several disciplines, traumatic stress incorporates such other areas of study as: post-traumatic stress disorders (PTSD), victimology, suicidology, stress and coping, Nazi Holocaust studies, disaster studies, bereavement studies, crisis theory/intervention, stress-management studies, learned-helplessness studies, and the study of victims of rape, abuse, and other types of violence (Wilson, Harel, and Kahana (eds), 1988). A useful, albeit quite general, definition of stress is any demand that disrupts homeostasis, and thus taxes the individual's adaptive resources (Monat and Lazarus, 1977). In turn, coping, as a response to the disequilibrium of a stressful state, has been viewed as the successful reduction of stress. In this conception, coping involves the re-establishment of homeostasis, mainly in the cognitive appraisals made by the victim. However, Hobfoll (1989) provides a critique of this view in which he argues that homeostatic models overemphasize people's phenomenology in deference to consideration of environmental resources (for example, whether or not a cancer victim is living alone or with someone – with the latter facilitating coping).

The psychological effects of severe stress are varied and at times even contradictory in nature, but may include: psychic numbing, anxiety, depression, intrusive unpleasant imagery, nightmares, exaggerated startle responses, disturbed sleep patterns, guilt (often in a form called "survivor's guilt" and self-condemnation), impaired concentration or memory, and fear and avoidance of situations that remind the individual of the stressful events. These are classic PTSD symptoms and may result not only from combat experience, but also from a host of traumas such as rape and incest. Social psychological effects may also be evident, such as interaction patterns that involve aggressive conduct or other dysfunctional and/or anti-social activity. Further, the individual may come to feel no rapport with others, even close others, resulting in little self-disclosure regarding these states of inner turmoil. How long do such effects last? They may last a lifetime, or they may dissipate within months. Many Vietnam veterans have suffered the effects of PTSD for over two decades, with total healing nowhere in sight; while the sudden death of a child is a matter that continues to affect a parent to the grave, though the nature of the grief may change over the years.

Lifton (1988) suggests that, in its simplest form, the traumatic syndrome can be defined as the state of being haunted by images that can neither be enacted nor cast aside, and that suffering is associated with being "stuck." Bergman and Jucovy (1982) have identified three ways survivors react to the Holocaust: (1) living as if the Holocaust is still a current reality; (2) trying to repress the memories of the Holocaust; or (3) attempting to sublimate through writing and speaking about the Holocaust, to keep its memory alive. In the following section, we shall argue that whether dealing with the Holocaust or other traumatic events, people often cope via account-making about the whys and wherefores of the events. While sometimes account-making may represent the type of sublimation Bergman and Jucovy note to be occurring in these writing and speaking activities, we would argue that it also may be directly and explicitly aimed at restoration of functioning in the mind of the account-maker. Returning to Monat and Lazarus's definition of stress, an implication of our argument is that homeostasis in the psyche is possible only if public or private account-making has occurred. We would agree with Hobfoll (1989) about the importance of environmental conditions as critical to the promotion of coping. Account-making can not be effective if it is not accompanied by facilitating external conditions, such as a caring close relationship.

A THEORETICAL MODEL OF ACCOUNT-MAKING UNDER SEVERE STRESS

In an analysis that can be related usefully to account-making, Horowitz (1986) proposed that the normal phases of stress response syndromes involve, in order, a stressor event; a person's outcry such as display of fear, sadness, or rage; and then the development of denial, intrusion (unwanted thoughts of the event), working through reaction to the stressor, and completion. When in this sequence is account-making most likely to occur? It may occur at any point, but it is most likely to develop in fragments at the denial phase and be ongoing in the phases of working through and completion. It is at the working-through stage that we propose the most intensive account-making will occur – that is, where the most intensive and extensive asking of "why" questions and development of theories of causality and responsibility will occur. Marmar and Horowitz (1988) describe the individual who is succeeding at the working-through phase as growing in capacity to contemplate memories of the event, experience emotions, revise distorted meanings, and plan for the future. The person at this phase can better tolerate the implications of the event and put these working-through experiences aside at times in order to engage in practical aspects of living. We shall mention completion needs again (pp. 59–60), but at this point, it should be emphasized that the completion phase represents success in working through the stressful event. This phase also implies learning and skill development based on the process of dealing with the stressor.

Most of the empirical work that has been done on account-making has focused on people's early cognitive-emotional reactions about recent events (Weiss, 1975), or on people's retrospective reflections about events in their lives (Weber, Harvey, and Stanley, 1987: a study of the accounts given by older adults enrolled in summer Elderhostel courses). We know too little about whether or not account-making differs across stress-response phases. We might predict that it would be fragmented and simplistic early in the sequence, but then become more coherent and refined later, as in the working-through and completion phases.

In another model of life crisis and transition, Moos (1986) proposes a set of stages that corresponds to working-through and completion. These are cognitive appraisal (which involves perceiving the meaning of an event) and adaptive tasks. The classic work of Lazarus (1966) has been informative in pinpointing the role of cognitive appraisal as a frequent step in stress responses. We suggest that account-making subsumes the appraisal activities and may serve as one type of adaptive task embarked upon at some point in the sequence.

In discussing this stress-reaction sequence and the place of account-making in it, we do not contend that all survivors go through this sequence. Rather, the sequence represents an idealized scheme. We prefer to emphasize account-making activity, in the story-like fashion we have outlined, over simple attributional activity or cognitive appraisal, because account-making relates well to the *fullness* of the narrative that the survivor will develop and is more faithful, we believe, to the *naturalistic* character of the survivor's interpretive activity.

It should be noted at this point that we are including in the category of "stressor events" a broad spectrum of experiences.

These events may include major trauma, such as the sudden death of a loved one; the loss of one's job; separation or divorce; the experience of rape or incest; being publicly accused of a major moral impropriety; and undergoing transitions such as the advent of a mid-life crisis or an identity crisis at the time of retirement. Certainly, account-making may differ according to type of event, but at this point we think that it is important to theorize in an inclusive fashion about the possible set, and await the empirical work that will differentiate these associations.

Our model of account-making as a process in the stress-reaction sequence is presented in figure 3.1. It is a major revision of Horowitz's (1986) model, adding emphasis on where account-making will enter the normal reaction pattern, and what might be the likely consequence of failure to engage in account-making during the later stages of the sequences. We have added the component of identity or self-concept change as the final step in the sequence. We believe that such change is related to the nature of the account that the survivor develops. For example, an account that presents self as "previously a timid and dependent wife who, in coping with and overcoming the loss of a husband and family income, became an aggressive, adroit businessperson" is one type of account that will be related to a stable identity change. The account may operate as part of a self-perception (Bem, 1972) by the account-maker/survivor ("Look at all that I have gone through; I now can handle anything"), even as it may influence close others to change their view of the survivor. Other types of accounts may be related to a much lesser degree to a stable identity change. Kurt Vonnegut suggested in his novel *Mother Night* (1966) that we are what we pretend to be; thus, we must be careful about what we pretend to be. A perceptive corollary added to this line by Shotter (1987) is that we must also be careful about the stories we tell ourselves since we may become what they say about us. Whether the account is correlative or causal in an identity-change process, we believe that it is a central device in informing self and other about the change.

As can be seen from figure 3.1, we argue that possible negative consequences of failure to engage in account-making during the later stages of the stress-response sequence include a gamut from anxiety-hypertension to prolonged grief, to failure, to maladaptive response patterns. One of the only indirect programs available to support this conception has been carried out by Pennebaker (1985, 1989). His work shows that trauma victims who have not confided their traumatic experience and its personal consequences for them to close others are more likely to suffer from such long-term physical

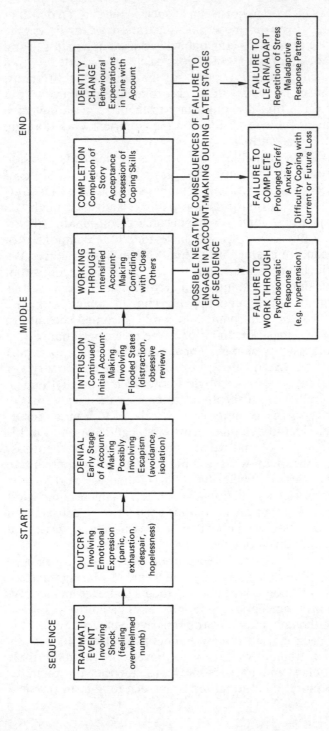

Figure 3.1   Model of occurrence of account-making in stress–response sequence

Source: Adapted from Horowitz, 1986, p. 41; also presented in Harvey, Orbuch, and Weber (in press).

problems as high blood pressure. While Pennebaker does not present a full statement on the nature of confiding, we would argue that at its core is the survivor's expression of what happened, why it happened, and his or her personal reactions to the event – in other words, an account. Such a position is supported in recent work designed to extend Pennebaker's paradigm by Murray, Lamnin, and Carver (1989). These investigators showed that brief psychotherapy, involving confiding an account to a caring other, led to relatively positive, emotional and cognitive effects for the account-maker.

It is also possible to construe work on PTSD among wartime survivors that reveals similar psychopathology as resulting partially from inadequate working through their memories and emotions. There is good evidence that account-making-type activity and cathartic expression is helpful in alleviating psychological problems for Vietnam War PTSD sufferers (Brende and Parson, 1985).

In the next section, we shall outline each of the major processes theorized to be associated with account-making. In so doing, we shall link the processes to aspects of psychological stress and coping.

PSYCHOLOGICAL PROCESSES ASSOCIATED WITH ACCOUNT-MAKING

Affect

The type of affect often associated with account-making for highly disturbing events is that of intense, negative feeling, or a feeling of lack of personal control. Early in the sequence, at the outcry point in our model, feelings of loss, being overwhelmed, or numbed by the event, and even feelings of despair and hopelessness are common. We suggest that such feelings will be followed by some type of behavior signifying either a cry of rage or an outcry for help. Essentially, this response is an energy-discharge, which can be considered instinctual in nature – unlearned, reflexive, survival-oriented, and triggered by specific circumstances. Taylor, Wood, and Lichtman (1983) provide a thoughtful discussion of such a response, which is often displayed in the accounts of persons who discover they have a life-threatening illness. In another statement on the role of emotion in accounts, Clarke (1987) suggests that affective "story-lines" run throughout close relationships. In this dialogue of the emotions between two people, over time many feelings reflecting more general states, such as devotion, disgust, or neglect, are reciprocally exchanged in myriad gestures and conversations.

Evidence relevant to emotions associated with accounts comes from literature on how children cope with the loss of a parent. This work suggests that emotional reactions in the immediate wake of a parent's death may determine life-long patterns of coping with intimacy and loss. Children will cope better and handle their grief more effectively, both at the time and later as adults, if they have both the opportunity and encouragement *to talk* about their feelings (Kranzler, 1988). Moreover, short-term and long-term coping reactions are more effective if bereavement is expressed as sadness rather than channelled into other emotions, such as fear or anger (Breier, in press). Such work on children's grief has important implications for the value of timeliness of affect accompanying account-making in the early stages of response to severe stress.

We shall cite two poems in their entirety because they illustrate well the different degrees of emotion that can be found in account-making. As we shall elaborate in chapter 7, poems and other literary works often serve as powerful conveyors of emotion – as well as of images and thoughts – in their depiction of some aspect of life. These poems show emotion occurring at later points in our model of when account-making occurs in response to severe stress. They suggest that affect is occurring in an influential way at the working-through stage and even into the identity-change stage. The first poem was written by a college student to her former boyfriend and published without by-line in the University of Houston student newspaper, in 1984. In its short but direct story, this poem conveys many images of happiness and then sadness – or "shades of blue," to use the writer's term:

Shades of Blue

A subtle passing
wouldn't do
– you touched me
and I noticed you.

Hand in hand
we walked a while
I'm forgetting how
you made me smile.

They said we were
a handsome two . . .
. . . you know,
I do believe it's true.

I'm better off
for knowing you.
– Still lingering on
are shades of blue.

The second poem reveals in its account-like form a crying out of great proportions. In its statement about the human condition, this poem shows a type of cathartic release about events that are devastatingly numbing and inhuman in nature. The poem was written by a nurse who served in Vietnam, and it was left at the Vietnam Veterans' Memorial, the great black granite wall in Washington, DC, as so many messages have been left by the grieving to their lost lovers and friends, whose names are inscribed on the wall. The reader is referred to Palmer (1987) for a set of revealing sketches of these notes, their writers, and the fallen comrades they write to and about; consider too that these messages reflect cathartic release processes on the part of the writer or account-maker, as well as self-presentations and morality laden testimonials to the unknown others who will read the messages. Regarding the cathartic value, in interviewing people who had left messages, Palmer says,

> People, I found, not only want to talk about the person they lost in Vietnam, they need to talk. It is a deep yearning in many, suppressed because of the wildly erroneous notion that by now they should be "over it." (1987, p. xiii)

I went to Vietnam to heal
and came home silently wounded
I went to Vietnam to heal
and still awaken from nightmares
about those we couldn't save.
I went to Vietnam to heal
and came home to grieve for those
we sent home blind, paralyzed,
limbless, mindless.
I went to Vietnam to heal
and discovered I am not God.

To you whose names are on this wall
I am sorry I couldn't be God.
If I were God, if there were a God,
there would be no need for such a wall.

But I am not God, and so I go on
seeing the wounded when I hear a
chopper, washing your blood from my hands,
hearing your screams in my sleep, scrubbing

the smell of your burned bodies from my clothes,
feeling your pain, which never eases,
fighting a war that never ends.

Dusty, Vietnam 1966–8
(cited in Palmer, 1987, p. 124)

MEMORY-COGNITION

Central to account-making are people's memories of the problematic event and their continued thinking about the event. We shall discuss memorial and cognitive activity about the past event here as a combined process. This process can be expected to become pronounced at the working-through and completion stages in our theorized model of response to severe stress. We believe that perceived control is a key facet of this process. Weiss (1975) outlines how people struggle to develop stories that provide them with a sense of control over the troubling events. These stories often involve a description of anticipated further consequences and plans for coping. Such stories may have script-like qualities. Scripts are hypothesized structures that organize a person's comprehension, and later guide performance (Schank and Abelson, 1977). As an illustration, the steps involved in seeking a divorce may have many scriptal elements, even as does relationship-threatening conflict (see Ginsburg, 1988, for an interesting analysis of scripts and relationships). Accounts may reflect a considerable degree of scriptal thinking and reporting because scripts provide what are usually simple answers and action plans for problems – whether or not the simple answers are effective answers.

Account-making for highly problematic circumstances often involves varying degrees of depressive thought, with unpleasant foci predominating in more severe depression. It may also involve obsessive thoughts, ruminations, and general worries (Tait and Silver, 1989; Wortman and Silver, 1989). Wortman and Silver's work, in particular, emphasizes the sorrow and depressed condition attendant on rumination without satisfaction about a highly distressing event. Horowitz (1986) describes the role of the completion tendency in people's use of thought to adjust to severe stress. He defines this tendency as the need to match new information with inner models based on older information, and the revision of both until they correspond. This tendency is similar to earlier ideas, such as Lewin's (1935) hypothesis about the importance of interrupted events in creating a tension and resulting completion-oriented drive state (the "Zeingarnik Effect", see p. 16 above), to G. Mandler's (1964, 1975) theory of how the interruption of plans and programs of action produces a negative emotional state, and to Berscheid's (1983) extrapolation of the completion hypothesis regarding emotion logic to apply to close relationship difficulties. Horowitz contends that until completion occurs, the new information and one's reactions to it are stored in active memory (and any accompanying depression or worry persists). Perceptions and immediate responses to serious life-events remain stored in active memory because, on first encounter, the meanings are recognized as having high personal relevance. Because the contents are strongly coded in active memory, they tend to be represented intensely and frequently. With each recurrence of the information, the comparisons are made again, and the emotional activation increases. In terms of the dynamics that mediate completion tendencies in account-making, Horowitz's reasoning implicates strongly the role of vivid memories and imagery for events that have not been adequately understood and/or cognitively-emotionally worked through by the account-maker.

What type of memorial trace is principally at work in account-making? We believe that it is what Tulving (1983) has referred to as episodic memory, defined by the unique, concrete, personal experiences dated in the rememberer's past. Most accounts appear to be composed of numerous episodic representations that people continue to experience in flashbacks and use in developing further semantic contexts for the accounts. These types of personal or autobiographical memories (D. C. Rubin, 1986) may remain highly vivid over time, having qualities similar to what Brown and Kulik (1977) have called "flashbulb memories." We have studied such memories and their association with current psychological states in close relationships (Harvey, Flanary, and Morgan, 1986). One finding from this research was that for women, high depression (as measured by Beck's (1967) instrument) was associated with a high degree of reported vivid memory of negative events pertaining to a past close relationship. Also, both men and women reported highly vivid and detailed memories of the beginnings (including first sexual encounter) and endings of relationships. As Neisser (1982) suggests, the events spotlighted by vivid memories may have a special benchmark function in people's memory of their personal past, even as our memories of events (e.g. President Kennedy's assassination) serve such a function in the collective memory of a nation or group of people. This landmark quality of some memories is eloquently reflected in the following scene from Campbell Armstrong's novel *White Light*, which focuses on the first love-making episode between the two protagonists in the story:

Pagan kissed her, and warmth of the kiss, the confident way she returned it, shook him. He undid the buttons of her shirt and slid his hand over a breast and saw how she raised her face back and upward, her mouth open and her throat in shadow, and it was one of those sublime perceptions he knew would return years later even after this passion had gone, one of those pictures that are immediately luminescent in the memory and against which other encounters are inevitably judged. (1988, p. 260)

We believe that the memorial part of accounts for events of stature in our lives often contains many such vivid memories. And although they may fade over time, the essence of such memories probably stays with us until death. Indeed, eventually many of us may put the finishing period on our master-account by reference to such pictorial and poignant snapshots in the mind.

The memory-cognition component of account-making involves the potential for reconstruction of events (Bartlett, 1932). One's retrospective "dredging up" of what happened in the past no doubt is somewhat affected by current beliefs and feelings, and may map on to what actually happened only to a small degree. As Robbe-Grillet (1986) observed, memory sometimes belongs to imagination; it is part of the imaginative process. Some of the most interesting contemporary work on reconstructive memory is being done by Ross, McFarland, and colleagues (McFarland and Ross, 1987; Ross, 1989). They propose, for instance, that people use the present to serve as a benchmark for their past regarding some personal attribute (for example, how depressed they were six months ago) because the present is more salient and available in memory than is past standing on that attribute.

Let us conclude this section with some comments about the great sustaining force of one's thoughts, memories, and emotions as they pertain to his or her understandings and buffer the effects of outside stimuli. In the following quote, Frankl (1963) eloquently examines processes that are quite similar to the combined forces of cognition, emotion, and memory in account-making that we have discussed. He shows how these processes helped him cope with the stresses of his internment in a Nazi concentration camp:

. . . the man marching next to me whispered suddenly, "If our wives could see us now!" . . . . That brought thoughts of my own wife to mind. And as we stumbled on for miles, slipping on icy spots, supporting each other time and again, dragging one another up and onward, nothing said, but we both knew: Each of us was thinking of his wife . . . . Then I grasped the meaning of the greatest secret that human poetry and human thought and belief have to impart: *The salvation of man is through love and in love.* I understood how a man who has nothing left in this world still may know bliss, be it only for a brief moment, in the contemplation of his beloved . . . . For the first time in my life I was able to understand the meaning of the words, "The Angels are lost in perpetual contemplation of an infinite glory." This intensification of inner life helped the prisoner find a refuge from the emptiness, desolation and spiritual poverty of his existence, by letting him escape into the past. (1963, pp. 56–9)

Fyodor Dostoevsky also spoke of the power of such an inner life in *The Brothers Karamazov*, when one of the characters notes that a recollected moment in which a person has tasted life could be forceful enough and filled with sufficient charge that it could enable the person to survive many other moments.

BEHAVIORAL EXPECTATION

We believe that people begin to form expectations about future behavior based on their accounts for the past, mainly at the final stages of completion and identity change in the stress-response sequence. Indeed, the new self-identity that we posit to be often given momentum by account-making in the context of major stress can be realized only via new plans for behavior and new behavioral patterns (a logic that again is somewhat similar to Bem's (1972) cogent reasoning on the role of behavior in influencing self-perception).

What evidence exists about the relation between accounts and expectations for future behavior? Harvey et al. (1989) argue for, and provide some data to support, the position that people's accounts of past relationships are related to and may even determine future expectations for relationships. For example, it was found that among college students a type of explanation for a past break-up that emphasized a too rapid movement to intimacy was highly positively correlated with a future behavioral expectation of "going (more) slowly" in developing any subsequent relationship. In other words, if one's account of the last break-up explains the loss as due to hasty intimacy, one may resolve to move with less dispatch in future liaisons. We do not know if these respondents did in fact move more cautiously in their future relationships. But it seems likely that the expectation based on the past experience had some rippling effect on their future dating behavior. This type of finding is entirely consistent with our ideas about the function of accounts concerned with quest for control and understanding. As yet, however, we do not have evidence to show how the more subtle and complete types of accounts, which may be more prevalent in guiding people's lives, may be related to behavioral expectations or actual lines of action.

More generally, most of us are dreamers and are ambitious for our close relationships and life in general before we die. We may be at a stage in our relationship career where we still await "Prince Charming" or "Ms Perfect," or we may be at another stage in which we believe that someday we shall achieve a much closer relationship with our parents or lover. Such hopes and plans, we contend, often closely follow and parallel specific accounts, and in fact may evolve from them in a causal pathway of event→account→expectation. It is much easier, for example, for a person from a middle-class background and with nurturing parents to evolve a behavioral expectation of finding an optimal marital relationship early in adulthood, than it would be for a person who was raised in poverty and who did not know both of his or her parents. Thus, the story or account, however incomplete, may fuel the expectation for further action and social interaction, or it may provide its own vocabulary of motive (Mills, 1940) which then propels action.

McGhee provided this perceptive conclusion regarding the "empowerment" of accounts, i.e. as a stimulant of action: " . . . without such a reflexive appreciation of the ways worlds of experience come to be the way they are, we are prisoners, personally and scientifically, of an external and apparently inevitable present" (1987, p. 331).

A FUTURE RESEARCH AGENDA

In this final section, we shall present a brief set of hypotheses about the account-making process, which derives from previous work and the model presented earlier.

When

There are several lines of prediction that follow from our reasoning about when people will engage most intensely in the account-making process. We suggest that people will be highly involved in account-making associated with severely stressful events especially during the working-through phase of their reaction to the event. The unique suggestion of this hypothesis is that models that postulate *simple* cognitive appraisal or attributional steps may insufficiently characterize the process of effective coping during the working-through stage. That is, the more complete package of attributions and other material contained in the account may better reflect the depth and scope of people's coping activity. We hypothesize that a fuller account, which has probably had the input of close others (see below) and which has been refined over time, will be necessary for enhanced mental and physical health in the wake of the stressful event.

We also believe that account-making will intensify during periods when major transitions are possible (e.g. mid-life crisis, change of career, retirement, imminent death of a parent). This area is particularly ripe for research in light of the aging of the populations of many countries. For example, it may be predicted that account-making will be a salient activity as people enter their "golden years" and are still mentally agile, as Weber et al.'s (1987) evidence suggests. The desire to put one's affairs in order – including one's memories and life-story – may be highly pronounced during this period. As the newspaper columnist Bob St John observed: "Older people have great stories to tell. They seem to have reached the age where every time they tell a story it's as if it's for the first time" (*Dallas Morning News*, 12 February, 1989). The merit of studying account-making in the elderly may be facilitated by the increase in "reminiscence groups" and is revealed powerfully by recent works such as Myerhoff's (1978) ethnographic study, discussed in chapter 1. More generally, it is imperative that work be done that involves longitudinal assessment of accounts and psychological health before and after major transitions. Such work would better establish the causal role of account-making in influencing health and various psychological states.

Completeness

One of the most theoretically interesting types of prediction deriving from the foregoing analysis is that after traumatic events, people will exhibit fewer physical and psychological health problems to the extent that they have developed complete accounts. Why? We have already noted the tension-reduction possibility suggested by theorizing, such as that found in Lewin's (1935) field theory, and the idea that vivid memories or flashbacks may play a role if completion has not occurred. However, given the social character of most account-making, other mechanisms also may be proposed. A plausible one is uncertainty-reduction theory (Berger, 1979), which suggests that people engage in communication in order to predict and explain others' behavior and that their uncertainty about others' behavior is reduced by the information-exchange process. This position was refined with respect to close relationships in work by Albrecht and Adelman (1987), who emphasize network communication systems and talk as crucial to social support and health. Giles and colleagues (e.g. Giles, Williams, and Coupland, in press) have argued persuasively that the value of social support is enhanced when sociolinguistic parameters of support encounters are considered. Future work on the completion drive in account-making needs to evaluate these ideas about uncertainty reduction as well as sociolinguistic factors such as assumed status and roles of interactants. Such work too should begin to probe criteria of account completeness. We assume that among these criteria will be the account-maker's own feeling of satisfaction with the account's conclusiveness.

Who

This question pertains to who, in terms of demographic or personality variables, or gender, or other trait-like qualities, engages in most account-making, and in account-making that is most effective in addressing psychological and other problems. Relevant to these concerns is work on social memory which suggests that women may be more likely than their male significant others to take on the role of "relationship historian," and maintain a continuing effort to observe, document, and analyze major relationship events (Holtzworth-Munroe and Jacobson, 1985; Ross, 1988). Another trait-like variable that may relate to account-making or to how one perceives others' accounts is that of dispositional empathy (Davis, 1983). As before, the need for and potential value of longitudinal work on such questions cannot be overstated.

Themes

There are only a few clues available in the literature of account-making about the various themes per types of event that people may exhibit. In the work of Harvey et al. (1986) on reports of vivid memories for past relationships, depression was positively related to rated vividness and unpleasantness of memories. This evidence suggests that people who are still having trouble coming to grips with previous stressful events may experience frequent instances of episodic recall. While justification and exoneration of self are common themes in the marital separation and dissolution situation (Weiss, 1975), it is likely that mostly dyadic-causality themes predominate in the attributions of persons involved in satisfying relationships (see Fincham and Bradbury, in press; Jacobson et al., 1985, for such evidence that derives from impressive programs of research on marital satisfaction and marital interaction). Also relevant is the work on people's reactions to their own or significant others' development of life-threatening illness. The themes of "God's will" and luck of fortune are often reported by participants in these situations (Turnquist, Harvey, and Andersen, 1988). In general, we would predict that account themes emphasizing more discriminating causal analyses (e.g. complex answers for complex events) will be related to more positive psychological functioning (see related work on attributional complexity by Fletcher et al., 1986).

Account-making and Social Interaction

As the section on behavioral expectation implied, too little work has been done to link accounts and social interaction. When, for instance, will action directed toward other or self be clearly and directly based on accounts? Our earlier theorizing would predict that account-based action will begin in the working-through and completion phases. Questions may also be asked which parallel existing social psychological literatures: will reciprocity of accounts about highly personal matters occur as it has been found to occur for self-disclosure (Derlega, Margulis, and Wisntead, 1987)? In this vein, it is possible that sociolinguistic factors such as age and status may influence whether reciprocity occurs and/or the form it will take (see Coupland et al., 1988, for a provocative analysis of how such factors affect language use). Similar to work on attribution (e.g. Yarkin, Harvey, and Bloxom, 1981; Town and Harvey, 1981), will accounts be found to mediate social interaction by affecting interaction so as to enhance or diminish stereotypes that existed prior to the interaction? Town and Harvey reported that college students who believed that another person preferred a homosexual lifestyle wrote more negative attributions about that person on an impression formation task and then also showed more avoidant non-verbal behavior when interacting with the person than did college students who believed that the other person had a heterosexual lifestyle. Will a person's accounts about another person then affect later behavior in such a regulating fashion? In a study to examine this question, accounts would be story-like material produced by the person forming the impression, and not the more singular and often disconnected attributions produced by respondents in the work by Town and Harvey and other researchers in the attribution area.

In conclusion, the very potency of account-making that we postulate may be highly dependent upon social interaction. This possibility is one that begs empirical scrutiny if the accounts topic is to achieve its full promise as a key construct in the social and behavioral sciences. It is also related to the central issue of *to whom* important accounts will be communicated. Close friends and confidants (whether or not lovers) and the quality of interaction they provide for confiding and feedback on one's accounts may be crucial if the accounts are to ameliorate stress in the fashion we have suggested. The previously discussed work by Pennebaker (1985) and by Murray et al. (1989) on confiding and health supports such a view. This position is suggested by the film *Hanoi Hilton* which depicts how US prisoners of war in Vietnam survived the maltreatment and agonizing despair they encountered in a Hanoi prisoner-of-war camp. An article by Hank Whitemore (*Parade Magazine*, April 1987), who interviewed the ex-POW who was consulted in making this film, describes how a subtle type of account-making combined with exchanged confidances was essential to POWs' survival. This process involved intensive private thought and reminiscence (after the fashion described by Frankl, 1963) and sharing secrets, stories, and humor with other POWs by intricate, surreptitiously-devised communication systems, which sometimes did not involve a single utterance.

The writer Phillip Lopate describes in a telling way the value of an activity quite similar to account-making/confiding in his close friend during his mid-life:

> I remember a balmy Saturday afternoon in early spring when a good friend and I met at a cafeteria and talked for three or four hours . . . . Together we diagnosed our mutual acquaintances, each other's characters, and the way of the world. In the course of our meanderings, we descended into what was really bothering us. I learned about something preying on his mind that he had told no one else yet: that an old friend of his from college was dying. I told him of my worries about my father's poor health and my anxieties about the surgery my father needed. We had touched bottom – mortality – and it was reassuring to settle there awhile. Gradually we rose again, back to the questions of ego, career, craft, and romance . . . we ended up walking through a new mall in Houston, gawking at the window displays, happily curious about the world again, now that we had dwelt long enough in the shared privacies of our souls. (An Amigo of One's Own, *Texas Monthly*, Feburary 1988, p. 148).

Tobias Wolff makes a similar point in describing his close bond with the writer Raymond Carver, and says of their friendship: "But it wasn't staying up all night that made us friends, or being thrown together in peculiar circumstances. It was stories. Stories and storytelling" ('Raymond Carver had his cake and ate it too,' *Esquire* September, 1989, p. 244).

SUMMARY

In this chapter, we have presented a model of account-making under conditions of severe stress. We have contended that account-making occurs throughout the stress-response sequence, but that it is most coherent and refined toward the point when the person is working through his or her reactions. In presenting this argument, we have linked our ideas about account-making with the literature on the psychology of traumatic stress and discussed some of the central theses in that literature. This chapter has also discussed major psychological processes associated with account-making, and concluded with a discussion of promising research possibilities for future study. We next turn to a description of the beginnings of research on person perception and accounts. Do perceivers develop different perceptions of others based on different characteristics of the others' accounts? If so, what are those characteristics, and what are the theoretical dynamics behind such tendencies?

4 Person Perception Through Accounts

Standing at the water's edge, hemmed in by fog, she had been moved to open her suitcase and show him its contents. None of what she'd brought was much different from any other time. There were the usual two or three comic books, he recalled, and probably a snack for her sweet tooth – a squashed Hostess cupcake perhaps, with the frosting smashed into the cellophane – and of course the rhinestone hatband that had once belonged to their mother. And finally her greatest treasure: a fan magazine with Elvis Presley on the cover. King of Rock, the title read. Dorrie worshipped Elvis Presley, Ordinarily, Ira humored her . . . "Elvis," Dorrie said happily, and Ira said, "For God's sake, Dorrie, don't you know the guy is dead and buried?" Then she had stopped smiling and her eyes filled with tears, and Ira had felt pierced. Everything about her all at once saddened him – her skimpy haircut and her chapped lips and her thin face that was so homely and so sweet, if only people could see . . .

Anne Tyler, *Breathing Lessons*, 1988

November 6, Friday morning. The dreaded day has finally come. I write with a trembling hand. I have enjoyed a sweet, glorious, sublime season with my darling, my beautiful, the life of my heart, my existence. Without her I should not wish to live longer. I am going to leave this morning all that makes me happy, the woman for whom I live. What cruelty! Shall I ever see her again? I shall always hope.

Excerpts from Young Ward's Dairy (1935), written in 1863 during the US Civil War (Young survived); reprinted from Rosenblatt, 1983

The opening quotations in this chapter are presented to illustrate the pervasive tendency of people to present themselves to others in their public account-making. Whether people present themselves non-verbally and symbolically by the contents of a suitcase as in the first instance, or by a diary excerpt as in the second, these presentations often reveal much about the presenter and his or her qualities.

PERCEPTIONS BASED ON ACCOUNTS

Throughout the course of their lives, people interpret their behavior and construct stories that link together the central events and significant others in their lives. As reviewed in chapter 2, accounts and related concepts are providing a new venue for theorizing and research for investigators interested in how people give meaning to their lives. Whether the concept involved in these works was that of accounts or some related idea (e.g. narrative mode of knowing), the focus has been on a broad type of interpretation or story-telling as the central activity. In addition to the previously reviewed work, research by Trabasso and his colleagues (Trabasso and van den Broek, 1985; Trabasso, van den Broek, and Suh, 1988) has gone one step further and examined how these story-telling activities are recalled. These cognitive psychology scholars essentially have been concerned with basic memorial processes and to a minor degree with how people perceive others portrayed in stories. This work by cognitive scholars, as well as the burgeoning work on accounts using archival, correlational, and survey methods forms a strong foundation for the present program of work aimed at examining accounts as stimuli for person perception.

In light of the emergence of accounts and related topics, it seems appropriate to begin to examine the person-perception process associated with people's presentations of personal stories to others. This examination would go beyond the work of cognitive psychologists interested in stories and recall and of social psychologists interested in person perception, to focus on *how the account-maker is perceived by others* as a function of the story-telling presentation. This work should represent a contribution both to the person-perception and account-making literatures because it focuses on how perception is affected by *naturalistic* and *relatively complete* story-like construction. How will an individual be perceived who presents certain personal qualities and decisions in his/her account? Will those qualities and decisions influence a perceiver's liking for him/her, or the perceiver's interest in being associated with the presenter? If an individual confides his/her most personal stories to others, are there certain types of accounts that evoke empathy or a more positive evaluation of the account-maker? What specific characteristics of accounts do others respond to that form the basis of these evaluations? Our program of work is designed to address such questions.

How account-makers will be perceived by others has been examined *to a limited degree* by theorists concerned with self-disclosure processes (Jourard, 1971; Derlega, Wilson, and Chaiken, 1976). However, self-disclosure theorists have focused on matters such as whether brief self-disclosing statements (which we term "gists", in chapter 8) are reciprocated, and how much people are liked who disclose to different degrees, and/or to different audiences, and/or under varying circumstances. To our knowledge, self-disclosure researchers have not paid attention to people's reactions to others' more elaborate stories (accounts).

More generally, investigation of the person-perception process associated with account-making may add to our knowledge of the account-making process in three important ways. First, the investigation of the person-perception process associated with account-making may facilitate our knowledge of people's naive psychology (Heider, 1958) about the ascription of meaning. If a person attributes a certain meaning to an important personal event, we tend to "read between the lines" to learn about that person's character and to infer other traits to the person (Jones and Davis, 1965); at the same time, we may develop particular sentiments and behavioral dispositions toward the person. Further, if accounts include, among other qualities, self-reported personal characteristics, others may not even have to "read between the lines" to arrive at inferences of dispositions and characteristics about the account-maker.

Second, the investigation of the person-perception process associated with account-making facilitates movement of the investigation of account-making from the survey/diary or structured interview and strictly correlational approach to the experimental paradigm. By holding constant certain variables and manipulating others, we can assess the relevance of various characteristics of accounts to impressions of the account-maker. In general, movement to an experimental paradigm should enhance our understanding of causal relations in this segment of work on accounts.

Third, the meaning of objects and situations is often constructed through interaction with others (McCall and Simmons, 1978; Stryker, 1981). Thus, it is important to study the reactions of others *to* individuals as well as the responses of individuals to stress-inducing events. Social perceptions are another avenue by which we gain information about ourselves (Cooley, 1902: Mead, 1934). In fact, social perceptions can be so effective that they instigate a self-fulfilling process: from social perceptions, to self-perceptions, to behavior, to confirmation of social perceptions (Darley and Fazio, 1980; Snyder and Swann, 1978; Snyder, Tanke, and Berscheid, 1977). That is, social perceptions can create social reality. Given these assumptions regarding social perceptions, if an account-maker reports orally or in written form, accounts to others, these accounts may be refined, elaborated on, or changed in that social give-and-take (Harvey, Orbuch, and Weber, 1990). By gaining information on how others respond to the account-maker based on his/her account, we can acquire further knowledge on how the account relates to norms and other people's experiences regarding a variety of environmental circumstances.

Part of what we have presented in earlier chapters is speculation or suggestions about the functions and manifestations of accounts and account-making. This chapter will describe a general theoretical conception of account-making and person perception and then some early evidence on how the presented account affects an observer's perception of the account-maker. The reported work is merely suggestive of the breadth of hypotheses regarding accounts that may be tested using person-perception experimental designs. The chapter concludes with a brief discussion of implications of the findings for actual interaction between perceiver and account-maker as well as a suggested set of new directions for research in this area.

THEORETICAL CONCEPTION

Our theoretical conception of account-making and person perception parallels, in part, the model of communication and persuasion developed by Hovland, Janis, and Kelley (1953). Hovland et al. articulated classes of variables that may influence persuasion. These classes of variables were associated with the communicator (e.g. credibility), the communication (e.g. qualities of the message such as fear appeal), and the audience (e.g. individual differences such as self-esteem). Hovland et al. further posited a set of mediating processes related to learning theory, as it then was being formulated, to explain complex forms of social behavior. In particular, they viewed attention, comprehension, and acceptance, as well as the rewards contingent upon attitude change, as critical to the persuasion process.

We have adopted the same general class descriptions that Hovland et al. proposed for independent variables in our theoretical conception of account-making and person perception. We suggest that account-making as a stimulus property may be divided into variables associated with the account and how it is presented, the presenter of the account, and the audience. We diverge from the Hovland et al. model in our focus on sentiment directed toward the presenter as the primary dependent variable and in suggesting that the major types of mediating processes are cognitive in nature and include: (1) the audience's perceptions of the normativeness of the event (or how likely an event is to occur in a given situation), (2) their empathy with the presenter and the predicament described, (3) their perceived similarity with the presenter and/or the extent they perceive that a similar type of event has occurred or could occur in their lives, (4) their perception of threat to self or personal values created by the event described, and (5) their experience in relating to such presentations of accounts (e.g. experience in reacting to someone's story of grief regarding the loss of a loved one).

At this point in our discussion of this conception, we do not try to spell out all of the major hypotheses that may be proposed, based on the mediating processes, for relationships between principal independent and dependent variables. However, we would suggest that many predictions may be derived from this conception. For example, as we describe below, in one study, we have tested whether the distress associated with an account affected liking for and trait inferences about the presenter. Our conception suggests that empathy would be one mediator of this effect, and we would anticipate that the direction would be toward more liking and positive evaluation the more distress exhibited. Before turning to brief reports of the first studies that we have conducted in this program, we summarize below the main aspects of our conception of account-making and person perception.

Classes of Important Independent Variables

1 Qualities of the *account* and how it is presented (e.g. the theme, causes of the event inferred by the account-maker, complexity of the account, whether or not emotion and other personal feelings are exhibited while communicating the account).
2 Qualities of *presenter* (e.g. credibility, gender, age).

3 Qualities of the *audience* (e.g. credibility; gender; age; type of relationship between presenter and audience, such as friends, close others, strangers or persons apt to be empathic with the account).

Classes of Important Dependent Variables

1 *Liking* (e.g. self-reported sentiment toward the presenter, or less direct expression of liking such as willingness to listen to the presenter describe at greater detail the account, or more generally, to do a favor for the presenter).
2 *Trait inferences* (e.g. evaluations of the presenter's maturity, sincerity, kindness, morality).

Important Processes Theorized to Mediate the Independent–Dependent Variable Relationships

1 Audience's perception of *normativeness* of the event described.
2 Audience's degree of *empathy* with the presenter.
3 Audience's degree of perceived *similarity* with the presenter and/or their perception that a similar event has occurred or could occur in their lives.
4 Audience's degree of perceived *threat* created by the events described.
5 Audience's degree of *experience* in relating to the events described.

EMPIRICAL WORK

We now trace the highlights of two empirical studies that have been completed thus far in this program of work on accounts and person perception (Orbuch, Harvey, and Russell, in presentation). The general procedure used in both experiments was an experimental person-perception design, containing manipulations of the independent variables within an experimental account-like written scenario. In these studies, a stimulus person presented an account of the breakdown of his/her marriage. In giving the story, the presenter either indicated that the breakdown of the marriage was partially caused by him/her engaging in an affair, or did not give such a reason (fidelity manipulation); the presenter also displayed either high or low distress following the break-up of the marriage (distress manipulation). We selected these independent variables for our first two studies because of their frequent operation in real-world account reporting (e.g. as in daily conversations between good friends regarding their close relationships and between characters in popular, continuing drama on television).

Further, in designing these studies and selecting the designated independent variables, we assumed that certain types of presented accounts may be more or less *acceptable* to perceivers if they judge the presenter's behavior as normative in terms of the situation described (with greater liking expected, the more normativeness perceived). Specifically, we assumed that a presenter who was generally similar in age to the subjects and who had recently completed college and embarked upon a business career would be seen as acting in a counter-normative way by engaging in an affair early in marriage. Therefore, we predicted that perceivers would exhibit the greatest disliking and attribute the least positive traits to presenters who reported having engaged in an affair. In contrast, we expected to find the most positive traits and the greatest liking for the presenter in the condition in which the person did *not* report an affair.

It was also assumed that the exhibition of great distress would be viewed by perceivers as more normative when a close relationship ends. Thus, it was anticipated that an account containing high distress would produce greater liking for and more positive traits ascribed to the presenter than would an account containing low distress. Overall, we predicted main effects for infidelity–fidelity (with less liking for infidelity) and distress (with more liking the greater the distress).

What about the gender of the perceiver? The respondents in both studies were male and female college students. In general, we know that gender differences have been found to be pervasive throughout the domain of close-relationship phenomena (Peplau, 1983) and in the particular area of accounts research (Harvey, Wells, and Alvarez, 1978). We assumed that male and female perceivers would differ in their reactions to presenters depending on whether the presenter was a male or female, with greater empathy, and thus greater liking, exhibited by females in general (Rubin, 1983). In Experiment 1, the presenter in all conditions was a female. In Experiment 2, the stimulus person in all conditions was a male. Gender of the presenter was the only variable differentiating the two experiments.

THE STIMULUS ACCOUNT

In the written and verbal instructions, we told the respondents that they would be reading a story another individual had disclosed to his/her close friend about his/her personal relationship. Respondents were told to read the account carefully and that afterwards they would be asked to give any impressions they may have formed based on the details of the story presented. Respondents were randomly assigned to one of the four experimental conditions. The basic stimulus account read as follows:

Joe and I met in college when I was 21 years old. I was majoring in English and he was in the school of engineering. I saw him talk in one of my psychology classes, and thought he was really good looking. The professor assigned us to small groups to evaluate the merits of a research study, using the research concepts we had learned in class. I can remember how excited I was to learn that Joe and I were in the same small group. We met a few times after class, and before I knew it, he asked me to a movie over the weekend.

The two of us really got along. We enjoyed doing the same things, talked about the same issues, and our friends even liked each other. After the two of us graduated, we decided to move to Chicago. Joe had a job with a major computing firm in the area, and I had accepted a job with a textbook publishing company. My parents live in Chicago, so we also had a chance to see them a lot. My parents really liked Joe, and that was important to me. In December of 1982, we decided to get married. Although we had each just started new jobs, and things seemed crazy at the time, we thought that we could provide each other with the social support needed during this hard and stressful time. We bought a house in one of the suburbs. My parents helped us with the down payment. We accepted their help. We knew that we would be able to pay the money back to them eventually, because of our potential dual income. The first three years were great! We would work hard during the week, and then go do things together on the weekends. We even tried to plan at least two trips a year. My parents continued to really like Joe, and he seemed to really like may parents. He even became best friends with my brother who also lived in a western suburb of Chicago. During the fourth year of our marriage, however, things became strained. We began to enjoy different activities and friends, and some different values emerged that I thought were important. He began spending more time at work. He did not take time off from work anymore to spend time with me. I also began spending more time in my office, and began working late hours and over the weekends. We basically began to move apart.

In the fifth year of our marriage, I had an affair with another man. I met the man at a workshop that focused on publishing books for children. We had so much in common, plus the fact that we both worked in the same general area. I felt close to this man. I felt so distant from Joe. Joe found out about my affair from another person in my office. It was at this point that Joe and I began to talk about our issues, and decided that we had grown apart, so much so that we couldn't repair the relationship that once was so important to each of us. We had changed. We tried to work things out. We even went to a marriage counselor to see if we could work out our differences. We had one session with the counselor, but it was a disaster. We tried to find some activity that we could share. I suggested we start a garden, but he never liked gardening. He suggested that we take a bridge class, but I wasn't good at cards. We discovered that about the only thing we had in common was eating, so we decided to go to dinner once a week. The idea was that we would have an evening all to ourselves that was special, but either we didn't have anything to say, or what we did have to say just created an argument. The whole thing was a disaster. At the end of that fifth year, we decided to separate. Joe moved into an apartment nearer to the place he worked, and I stayed in the house we had lived in together. After six months, we filed for a divorce.

I grieved for a while, and then began patching up my life. After several months, I began taking a mini-course in French at the university extension program, just to get out of the house. I have met other people in my French class. I don't know if I will ever completely lose the desire to want to be back in Joe's life, but I know that time heals the pain. Right now, though, I feel very lonely. I still have a hard time eating alone in the house we once shared, because the memories overwhelm me. There are even nights that I wake up at two or three o'clock in the morning, unable to sleep because I desperately want to talk with Joe or feel his presence. There have been days where I just sit and cry. The tears are hard to stop. At these moments, I feel helpless, and wonder if only we could have tried a little bit harder. My work has also suffered because I sit and daydream at my desk.

(In this example the stimulus person is female, admits an affair, and reports high distress.)

In this example, the presenter (Mary) offers an account of the breakdown of her marriage. In giving her story, Mary indicates that the breakdown of her marriage was facilitated by her engaging in an affair. In the fidelity conditions, the same story was told without the part involving Mary's (Joe's) affair with another man (woman). Instead, the couple is said to have drifted apart because of differences. Further, in the above example, Mary reports high distress following the breakdown of her marriage. In the low distress conditions, Mary (Joe) notes the same events but indicates that these feelings are not intense or long in duration, and that she (he) is beginning to feel better about the ending of the relationship and beginning to meet new friends.

Experiment 1: Results

Effectiveness of the manipulations   A manipulation check reveals that respondents were differentiating appropriately between the high/low distress conditions. We also obtained some evidence about the effectiveness of the infidelity/fidelity manipulation by examining respondents' replies to the question, "How responsible was the presenter for the breakdown of her marriage?". We assumed that respondents would attribute greater responsibility to the presenter for the breakdown of the marriage in the infidelity versus the fidelity conditions. The data support this assumption.

Perceived likability   Perceived likability of the stimulus person was assessed by a one-item measure of respondents' replies to the question, "How much would you personally like to know the presenter?". A seven-point scale (1–7, with high numbers indicating greater likability) accompanied the question.

An analysis of variance[1] revealed significant main effects for the variables of fidelity/infidelity and gender of perceiver. As predicted, respondents reported greater liking when the presenter did not engage in an affair. Also, female perceivers reported greater liking than male perceivers. This latter finding may stem from females' relatively greater empathy with a female presenter.

A significant three-way interaction among fidelity, distress, and gender of respondent qualifies the main effects. In general, males reported the greatest liking for a female presenter who revealed high distress and infidelity, whereas a female presenter who revealed low distress and infidelity produced the greatest disliking. On the other hand, females had the greatest liking for a female presenter who revealed high distress and fidelity; whereas, similar to the male perceivers, a female presenter who revealed low distress and infidelity produced the greatest disliking.

The data for this three-way interaction indicate that for both males and females, a female presenter who exhibited infidelity and low distress produced the greatest disliking. Further, female perceivers were more likely than males to use the standards of faithfulness and high distress when evaluating whom they liked the *most*. Males may especially like females who are unfaithful and highly distressed, because these females represent an available yet vulnerable partner to them. In other words, a woman judges another woman in terms of the other's being a friend (and is likely to be more empathic), but a man judges the woman in terms of a potential partner for him.

In sum, as expected, it was found that qualities of an account such as the presence of fidelity (cause of the event inferred by the account-maker) and high distress (whether or not emotion and other personal feelings are exhibited while communicating the account) affect whether an audience will like the account-maker. Further, the effect was different depending on whether the audience was male or female. This latter result suggests that males and females may place differential importance on what qualities are acceptable for females to present in their accounts, possibly because observers have different role expectations regarding the gender of the account-maker.

Inferred trait-like qualities   Respondents in the study were also asked to rate the stimulus person on eight adjectives (trait-like qualities): likable, moral, trustworthy, self-esteem, kind, selfish, mature, and respectable (1 = not at all, 7 = very much, e.g. 1 = not at all likable, 7 = very likable). The mean score for these items was the dependent variable in the next set of analyses (the greater the mean, the more positive traits ascribed to the presenter). An analysis of variance revealed a significant main effect for fidelity (respondents assigned *higher positive* trait scores, on average, to those female stimulus persons who did *not* engage in an affair). Thus, respondents perceived those females who were faithful as more moral, trustworthy, mature, respected, etc. No further significant main effects or interactions were discovered.

   In sum, only one quality of the account, fidelity/infidelity (cause of the event inferred by the account-maker), yielded a significant effect on trait inferences assigned to the presenter. Consequently, the independent variables of fidelity/infidelity and high/low distress produced differential patterns of data for the dependent variables of liking and inferred trait-like qualities. Why this discrepancy occurred is not clear. It may be the case that the dependent measures of liking and trait inferences were differentially sensitive to normativeness and empathy concerns.

Experiment 2: Results

Effectiveness of the manipulations   Responses to the distress and responsibility questions were checked. Respondents correctly perceived that presenters in the high-distress conditions were experiencing a greater degree of distress than those persons in the low-distress conditions, and that presenters in the infidelity conditions had greater responsibility for the breakdown of the marriage than those persons in the fidelity conditions.

Perceived likability   Similar to Experiment 1, the same main effect predictions were hypothesized for the male presenter in regard to how much respondents would like to know the presenter. In addition, the same assumptions were made regarding differential reactions to a male presenter by male and female respondents.

An analysis of variance revealed a significant main effect for the variable of gender of perceiver. Regardless of the condition, females reported a higher mean of likability for the male presenter than did males. Neither of the independent variables was significant. Further, contrary to the results in Study 1, the data did not confirm a three-way interaction between fidelity, distress, and gender of the perceiver.

These results suggest that regardless of the nuances and manipulations in the account, the male presenter (Joe) must have displayed traits that appealed to females. Why might such a tendency be obtained? Just for a moment recall the stimulus account that was presented earlier in this chapter (p. 71–2). Imagine a male presenter named Joe giving the same account, rather than a female presenter named Mary. Surprisingly, the constant information presented in the account is very expressive, sensitive, and personal, especially for a *male* individual to be telling to a close friend. These characteristics hold true regardless of the experimental condition. We would argue that these special traits are why Joe received high likability ratings from female respondents regardless of the experimental condition. That is, Joe comes across not as an insensitive divorced male, but as an unusually sensitive, perceptive, and articulate man who reveals great trust for and confidence in his account-receiver. In the eyes of women who read his story, the salience of his qualities may overwhelm the problems of his recent break-up (see Rubin, 1983, for a related line of reasoning).

Inferred trait-like qualities   The mean score of the eight adjectives was again used as the dependent variable to examine perceptions of the account-maker. An analysis of variance revealed significant main effects for fidelity (higher positive trait scores to those males who did not engage in an affair) and for distress (higher positive trait scores to those males who displayed high distress). Thus, respondents perceived those males who were faithful and who displayed high distress as more moral, trustworthy, mature, respected, etc. No further significant main effects or interactions were discovered.

Similar to Experiment 1, qualities of the account such as fidelity/infidelity and high/low distress yielded differential patterns of data for the dependent variables of liking and the inferred trait-like qualities. For the dependent variable of liking, neither of the account qualities was influential. However, gender of the audience did affect perceivers' liking of the presenter (female perceivers displayed greater liking of the male presenter than did male perceivers). We argue that this is because females were attracted to the expressiveness and sensitivity displayed by the male stimulus person in all conditions, by the very fact of his retelling an account to a close friend.

On the other hand, when perceivers were asked to infer trait-like qualities to the male presenter, these ratings were affected by qualities of the account. Male presenters who revealed infideltiy (cause of the event inferred by the account-maker) and low distress (lack of emotion and other personal feelings while communicating the account) were ascribed lower positive trait scores, on average, than male presenters who revealed fidelity and high distress. Again, the theoretical explanation for these differences is unclear. Perhaps the dependent measures ask recipients of accounts to engage in distinctive activities that are differentially sensitive to normative and empathic concerns.

IMPLICATIONS FOR THE ACCOUNT-MAKING LITERATURE

In general, what are the implications of these findings for the account-making literature? As stated previously, investigation of the person-perception process associated with account-making may help us add to our knowledge of the account-making process in important ways. Let us now re-examine these goals in light of this developing line of research.

If an individual claims to attribute a certain meaning to an important personal event, are observers likely to develop certain sentiments and behavioral dispositions toward that individual? This current line of research shows great potential in beginning to answer the question of how people perceive and react to others who present various types of accounts about major events in their lives. The studies outlined above indicate that perceivers *react* to the account-maker and arrive at *inferences* of dispositions and characteristics about the account-maker, given specific qualities of the account, the audience (gender), and the presenter (gender).

Do the findings provide clear evidence for the normativenss assumption? Both experiments provide some evidence for the assumption that certain types of presented accounts may be more or less acceptable to perceivers depending on whether the stimulus person's behavior was or was not normative for the situation. But, depending on whether perceivers are asked to infer other traits to the account-maker or develop particular sentiments toward the person, the independent variables of fidelity/infidelity and high/low distress yielded differential patterns of data *within* and *across* studies. Therefore, a clear theoretical explanation of a single mediating process underlying these ascriptions is not possible. How these patterns support the normativeness and/or other assumptions will require more careful analysis.

The results also indicate that the genders both of the perceiver and the account-maker appear to be important as they relate to the nature of the account. This type of evidence points to the overeaching roles of one's social or reference group and the mores subscribed to in such groups in influencing reactions to others based on their accounts.

Given this latter reasoning, when presenting our accounts to others, do we choose certain friends who abide by norms that are consistent with the behaviors and attitudes in our accounts? That is, do we confide in others whom we know will react positively to our accounts? On the other hand, do we develop accounts (whether "true" or not) to fit the norms of our reference groups? These questions seem especially relevant given the work by Walster (1966) and others examining defensive attribution and threat to self issues that stem from perceived similarity between other and self.

Regardless of whether we seek out others who are attitudinally similar to us, or whether we produce accounts to fit the norms of a group, the above data may be taken to suggest that the *content* of our account, which we present to others, can have wide ramifications for how others react and see us. These data are consistent with work by Lerner (1980), which has examined reactions and dispositions inferred to victims in terms of the Just World Hypothesis. It is important, however, that research be designed to probe more directly these questions regarding how accounts affect not only person perception but also social interaction.

This line of research also facilitates movement of the investigation of an aspect of account-making research toward an experimental paradigm to assess various causal relationships in this field of study. The above experiments manipulated two independent variables to demonstrate that impressions of an account-maker can vary as a function of specific qualities in an account.

FUTURE EXPERIMENTAL DIRECTIONS

The empirical work presented in this chapter suggests the value of the accounts person-perception experimental design. This line of research differs from past person-perception studies because it uses the account (the target of the research) as the stimulus material. Most person-perception studies (Schneider, Hastorf, and Ellsworth, 1979) use the stimulus scenario as a *vehicle* to examine another social psychological concept (such as how physically attracted the respondent is to the stimulus person or how willing the respondent is to provide social support to the stimulus person). In addition, rather than using a brief scenario without much content, the present research uses a rich, personal, historical statement, elaborate in detail and naturalistic sentiments.

Nevertheless, there are several limitations to these first two experiments. First, these empirical studies have investigated only two qualities of an account: the absence or presence of distress following a relationship dissolution and the evidence of fidelity or infidelity. Real-life accounts contain many other qualities in addition to those investigated here that may affect how the account-maker is perceived and reacted to by the recipients of the account. For example, as suggested in chapter 5 (Account-making and Griefwork), what if the account contains language that consists of platitudes and euphemisms? Are we, the perceivers, likely to infer negative personal dispositions to the account-maker given these characteristics? What if the following sentence was presented in an account by a male who had experienced the dissolution of a close relationship: "I finally feel relieved and happy." Do we infer that this man never loved his partner, or that he was the partner who initiated the break-up? Do we as perceivers react to him in a different manner than if he had presented an account filled with pain and anguish? In sum, an individual may present several types of personal qualities and decisions in his/her account that affect how he/she is perceived; furthermore, these qualities may have implications for how we react toward the individual. Future research must address these possibilities (additional qualities of an account are suggested in the outline of our theoretical conception).

Second, these studies examined only one quality of both the audience and the presenter – gender. Further research should explore other qualities of the audience and the presenter that may influence how we perceive and react to account-makers, such as age

(Coupland et al., 1988) and credibility of the presenter and audience. Along these same lines, the foregoing experiments asked respondents to react to *strangers'* accounts. The person-perception process associated with people's presentations of personal stories to others may differ depending on the relationship between account-maker and recipient of the account. Future research should include experimentation in which respondents react to account-makers who are their friends, intimate partners etc., *as well as* report on their judgements and reactions to account-makers who are strangers as described here.

Third, as in other person-perception experiments, actual person-to-person interaction with the stimulus person is lacking in the present research. This lack of face-to-face interaction does not negate the relevance of the experimental findings, but respondents may react differently if they are actually interacting with another person. When individuals present accounts to another person in-person, perceivers may be influenced by other stimuli (e.g. posture, vocal tones, and facial expressions) (Ickes, Bissonnette, Garcia, and Stinson, 1990), in addition to the presentation of the story.

Finally, the foregoing experiments have not attempted to answer the question of how accounts and/or behaviors may change as a function of the reaction of others. Again, social perceptions may influence the self-perceptions of the account-maker, which in turn may affect his/her behaviors. Future research might easily employ manipulations within an experimental paradigm whereby presenters of accounts are given differential feedback regarding their own accounts of personal events, to examine whether such feedback indeed influences future accounts (and behaviors). Thus, the researcher could examine if accounts for the same event change after social feedback.

SUMMARY

In this chapter, we introduced a theoretical conception of account-making and person perception that is similar to the model of communication and persuasion developed by Hovland, Janis, and Kelley (1953). We argue that, like the persuasion process, there are classes of variables that influence the account-making and person-perception process. In accordance with this theoretical conception, we presented brief reports of two person-perception experiments. In general, our findings indicate that perceived likability and trait-like inferences attributed to an account-maker are influenced by: (1) qualities of the account, such as the cause of an event inferred by the account-maker (infidelity/fidelity), and whether or not emotion and other personal feelings are exhibited while communicating the account (high/low distress); (2) a quality of the presenter (gender); and (3) a quality of the audience (gender). We also discussed specific patterns of data.

Accounts, like other utterances, are not produced in a vacuum. They emerge in a social context, through the filters of both account-maker and receiver. In this chapter, we have offered evidence that accounts are interpreted by receivers in assessing the storyteller, perhaps with long-term consequences for any relationship between the account-maker and receiver. In the next chapter we shift focus to examine the account as formed and related in consequence of a relationship loss.

Part II
New Directions in Work on Account-making

This part of the book contains four chapters that illustrate some new directions in theory and research on account-making. The first chapter, chapter 5, examines griefwork and links this topic to account-making. Chapter 6 focuses on an evolutionary perspective on account-making. Chapter 7 probes themes in accounts presented in general literature. Finally, chapter 8 discusses further research, directions and limitations of current work. An important element of the final chapter will deal with the questions, "When do people consciously avoid engaging in explicit account-making and why?"

5   Account-making and Grief Work

Can I see another's woe
And not be in sorrow too?
Can I see another's grief
And not seek for kind relief?
           William Blake (cited in Morrell, 1988)

INTRODUCTION

In 1960 the writer C. S. Lewis lost his wife of only four years to cancer. Lewis's marriage to Joy Gresham Davidman had been the culmination of an intense friendship between the middle-aged, formerly confirmed bachelor and his younger, admiring fan. Very shortly after her death, Lewis began to keep a kind of journal of his feelings and thoughts in the empty pages of notebooks he found in their home. When months later he ran out of blank pages, he determined not to buy additional books to record his jottings, an acknowledgement that while grief itself might have no clear ending, one's *story* has – even if it be determined by so arbitrary a limit as having run out of pages. Lewis published this journal pseudonymously as *A Grief Observed* (1963) two years before his own death. Compelled perhaps to write out his own grief, the pages of Lewis's journal record his own ongoing musings and struggles, rather than a story of remembered love. Yet the story of their relationship is very much *present* between the lines and paragraphs of Lewis's diary, and occasionally emerges to illustrate an insight experienced in the midst of his grief:

> What was H. not to me? She was my daughter and my mother, my pupil and my teacher, my subject and my sovereign; and always, holding all these in solution, my trusty comrade, friend, shipmate, fellow-soldier. My mistress; but at the same time all that any man friend (and I have good ones) has ever been to me. Perhaps more. If we had never fallen in love we should have not the less been always together, and created a scandal. (1963, pp. 55–6)

And finally Lewis reflects on writing in the journal itself:

> I thought I could describe a *state*; make a map of sorrow. Sorrow, however, turns out to be not a state but a process. It needs not a map but a history . . . There is something now to be chronicled every day. Grief is like a long valley, a winding valley where any bend may reveal a totally new landscape (1963 pp. 68–9)

What is the role of one's story in grief and the recovery from grief? Is account-making a compelling part of the process of grieving? Must the account be shared – expressed in a social context – in order to become "real," or can a private understanding suffice as well to yield comprehension, assuagement, and closure?

Among the variety of stressful events that might trigger the coping and account-making sequence (reviewed earlier, pp. 48–9), relationship losses are surely among the most recognizably traumatic. In this chapter we examine the dimensions of relationship loss and subsequent grief, and explore the roles and functions of accounts and account-making therein.

GRIEF WORK

The word "grief" has the same roots as "grave" and "gravity," conjuring the quality of weight or heaviness. Those who grieve suffer figuratively from a "heavy heart," an apt if quaint description of the physical and emotional consequences of shock and depression. While it is tempting to speak of grief as an emotional *state* – ponderous but temporary, as in "your time of grief" – modern grief theorists argue that grief is best understood as a *process* with arguably many levels and permeations and no clear cessation or "cure." Rando, defining grief as the process of "experiencing the psychological, social, and physical reactions to [one's] perception of loss" (Rando, 1988, p. 11), both admonishes and encourages the reader:

As a griever, you need to appreciate the fact that grief is *work*. It requires the expenditure of both physical and emotional energy . . . [Y]ou must actively *do* things and undertake specific courses of thought and action to integrate and resolve your grief. (ibid., p. 16)

The term "grief work" was originally coined by the psychiatrist Erich Lindemann in 1944 (cited in Rando, 1988, p. 16); it captures the sense of tasks to be successfully completed in order for one to resolve grief and resume immersion in life – albeit a different kind of life, even a different identity, from the one understood prior to the loss.

Rando and other grief theorists (e.g. Staudacher, 1987; Rosenblatt, 1988) have observed that the concept of griefwork conflicts with popular cultural myths about grief, revealed in such comments as "Try to be strong" and "After all these months you should be getting over this." Across grief experiences, idiosyncrasy is the rule. There are no "shoulds," no two identical patterns of grief. Complex conditions make each person's grief, like his or her former relationship with the lost individual, unique and distinct. None the less, cutting across so many individual worlds of pain, grief theorists have observed a pattern, a common sequence of three stages of grief: avoidance, confrontation, and re-establishment.

In the initial *avoidance* phase, when news of the loss has just been received, one's efforts are devoted to escaping the terrible acknowledgement of loss. Language may be reduced to outcry ("No! No! No! No! No!"), repudiation ("You've made a mistake, Officer, this is not my daughter"), or dazed utterance ("I cannot feel anything. This must be a dream") (Rando, 1988). In reacting to an unanticipated loss, one may fall into the grotesque ironies of informal chatter: "You're kidding!" (Viorst, 1986). We recoil from reality and plead for a return to the much better world of a few years, a few seconds ago: "The happy past restored. And that, just that, is what I cry out for, with mad midnight endearments and entreaties spoken into the empty air" (Lewis, 1961, p. 29).

The second stage of grief, *confrontation*, is better understood as an ongoing process of painful adjustment and realization than as a distinct phase or stage. In its most intense, early manifestations, it appears as "angry sadness," an unrelenting mourning for life possibilities – for what never was and now never will be, as well as for what was but will never be again. Anger and guilt cycle together in a spiral of self-recrimination and sorrow. Viorst offers a familiar litany of such expiations:

> "I should have been kinder."
> "I should have been more grateful for what I had."
> "I should have tried to call my mother more often."
> "I should have gone down to Florida to visit my Dad."
> "He always wanted a dog, but I would never let him have one, and now it's too late." (Viorst pp. 269–70)

A related manifestation of confrontation is found in the re-working of the griever's memories of the lost loved one, especially in the direction of what Viorst calls canonization ("My wife was a saint") or idealization ("My father was wiser than Solomon"). Such reconstructive retrospection has important implications for account-making, especially as it draws in other motives (e.g. self-justification, impression management) than grief work. (Review the discussion of the memory-cognition function of account-making, in chapter 3: Recollections of the lost partner or relationship are returned to and repeatedly compared, even contrasted, with new understandings and insights. Mismatches and clarifications are incorporated into both the memories themselves and the account-making process whereby they are focused and presented for oneself and others.)

The third phase of grief, *re-establishment*, is less a marked phase than a gradual change in the degree of grief. Sorrow and anger decline as the mourner makes a slow reentry into the everyday world.[1] Though still in mourning, the loss is "put in a special place." Grief waxes, wanes, and continues, but the mourner surfaces more and more frequently into the largely non-grieving world and the somehow-different light and atmosphere of a non-grieving consciousness. Accounts of grief will often in fact describe sudden resurgences of grief – what Rando (1988) calls "grief spasms" and Parkes (1972) calls "pangs" – as coming in "waves," and with other aquatic metaphors about immersion, drowning, gasping for air, or treading water. Such language is consistent with the sense of not just movement or progress, but surfacing, being borne upward toward the light and air.

Sometimes grief spasms occur as a result of unconscious, automatic habits of thought or action, as in this comment by a 54-year-old woman whose mother had died a few months earlier: When I am in the kitchen, I think I will have to tell her something—and then I realize she is not there."[2]

The grieving sometimes voice wonderment about whether they will ever be able to be "normal again." Given the universality of grief and mourning, the essential humanness of the "great leveler," it is ironic that anyone should consider a life to be "normal" that is free from loss or grief. Grief is surely as normal as love and intimacy, and probably as inevitable. In his own grief journal, C. S. Lewis observed that he was "aware of being an embarrassment to everyone I meet," but that

> To some, I'm worse than an embarrassment. I am a death's head. Whenever I meet a happily married pair I can feel them both thinking, 'One or other of us must some day be as he is now'. (1963, p. 11)

Love is thus a precondition of grief: Weiss (1988) observes that, while we form many instances and kinds of primary relationships, it is only our *relationships of attachment* whose loss triggers grief. A key distinction between attachment relationships and other primary relationships is the linkage of the former with feelings of security. Whereas the loss of a *community relationship* – e.g., a friend or colleague – may leave one with feelings of marginality and ostracism, in contrast the loss of an attachment figure leaves one with a keen sense of abandonment. The pain of such a loss, according to Weiss, may defy expression or understanding. Ultimately, then, grief is an individual experience, whose truth cannot be shared – any more than one can "share" the euphoria of falling in love. Our language, like funerals and other social conventions, provides at best a vehicle to bring together, to one time and place, what otherwise remain largely inarticulable, utterly private and separate personal realities. When we mourn "together" we mourn alone, in each other's company. Is the company of others an unpleasant or unnecessary consequence of custom? Or do our social rituals and exchanges offer a forum, a crucible, for these otherwise unvoiced agendas of loss?

RESOLVING GRIEF

The "work" of grief may then concentrate on two agendas: an intrapsychic or private quest for meaning and acceptance; and a more public (to degrees) processing and restructuring of the loss in both identity and social network. How are these agendas balanced and addressed? Initially, this may depend to some extent on whether the loss was *physical* or *symbolic*. Rando (1988) distinguishes between physical losses, in which something tangible has been made unavailable (e.g. a spouse dies, a car is stolen, or a house burns down), and symbolic losses, involving abstract changes in one's psychological experiences of social interactions (e.g., getting a divorce, losing status as a result of a job demotion, or losing a friendship after an argument). Rando warns that symbolic losses may not be recognized and so not accorded the grief and coping effort they deserve. As a result, the griever as well as others may fail to interpret grief over a symbolic loss as part of a normal and necessary adjustment. Thus the task of coping after a symbolic loss may first require accepting that there *has been* a loss, in addition to other objectives common to both symbolic and physical losses.

Whether the loss is physical or symbolic, several grief theories seem to agree that there are three processes necessary to "resolve" grief. First the bereaved person must acknowledge and understand the loss (Rando, 1988), or, in other words, accomplish *cognitive acceptance* (Weiss, 1988). The causes of the loss event must be understood and must comprise a satisfactory account. If there is any doubt about the reality or circumstances of the loss, these must be resolved and the loss confirmed. Thus the sudden death of a loved one in a distant locale – hearing that one's close friend or sibling has died while on an out-of-town trip, for example – may initially prompt more inquiries and red tape than grief. The symbolic loss when a partner or lover does not die but unexpectedly leaves and does not return may become disproportionately tragic because it seems senseless and unpredictable, and thus delays the grief of the one left behind. Rando (1988) maintains that one's account of the causes of a loss need not necessarily be "true" or the same as others' explanations, but it must satisfy the bereaved person, and provide a context and rationale for the loss. This concurs with our own conviction in the present discussion that the accuracy or verifiability of an account is less important (perhaps not important at all) than its subjective completeness and the closure it offers the account-maker.

The second general process necessary to "recovery"[3] requires experiencing the pain and reacting to the separation (Rando, 1988), or achieving *emotionai acceptance* (Weiss, 1988). Rando argues that "very simply, there is no way around" experiencing the pain of the loss. Weiss emphasizes that painful memories and associations must be confronted emotionally so that they can be "neutralized." One mark of progress in this direction is the diminished frequency with which the bereaved person examines alternative scenarios of past relationship events or circumstances of the loss iself – in other words, fewer self-assailing "if only's." Repressed or unexpressed feelings and memories cannot be faced or neutralized. If the bereaved person is allowed to compartmentalize the painful feelings, the effort necessary to "wall up" such potential intrusions may diminish the emotional possibilities of ongoing real life (Weiss, 1988). Thus, as difficult as it may be for both the bereaved person and his or her audience, the best form of social support may be that which encourages expression, and listens without judgment or advice (Vachon and Stylianos, 1988). It is at this point that we believe account-making may be most effective in the process of grief.

Consider the interactive function of "remembering out loud" in this 62-year-old widow's description of the days and weeks following her husband's death:

Neighbors who had known him slightly for only two years (we had moved from New York to Florida) rallied 'round. Many, many attended his funeral and mentioned that this was because of their caring for me. Friends brought in all our meals for the entire family for the five days we stayed at home in mourning. I am not at all religious, nor was Ira (he was cremated, against Jewish custom). But the gathering around, recounting stories about Ira, the emotional support was very important to me. I needed to know that others cared too and that I had this wonderful support system – people who stressed my personal strengths and growth – that would help in any way necessary. [4]

As social psychologists have found in classic research (e.g., Schachter 1959) on whether "misery loves company," it appears that misery does not want just *any* company. Grief, like misery, seeks the company of those who grieve likewise, or understand, or remember. The social-support role of account-making and account-sharing may be most obvious when it is *missing*. For example, successful grievers may take the presence of understanding co-grievers for granted, whereas those who have been less successful in coping will complain that no one was available to listen, or that those who listened did not really understand:

My friends were sorry but no one knew Mom for we live outside a large city where we do not know one another's parents.
(53 year-old homemaker.)[5]

The role of a widow is difficult to adjust to or adapt to. People's attitudes change – even close friends seem to draw back. They don't want to hear about him – if I mentioned his name, they would change the subject . . . I have not had anyone to talk to, except a professional social worker . . . And I wonder if anyone will read this long monologue? And what will "they" think?
(61-year-old retired social worker, concluding a seven-page response to a survey on coping with relationship loss.)[6]

Finally, the third essential process in "recovering" from close relationship loss involves adaptation to one's new life "without forgetting the old" (Rando, 1988), comprising a social *identity change*, based on a new self-image and an understanding that the lost relationship is now part of one's past rather than one's present. Rando recommends finding healthy ways of "keeping your loved one 'alive'" via remembered values, insights, and habits, and making sure others do not forget. Over the long term of grieving, this balance between the old life and the new identity may be facilitated by talking about the loved one (Staudacher, 1987; Rando, 1988), or even writing down one's feelings and memories about the relationship (Kingma, 1987; Staudacher, 1987). The goal of such verbal expression ultimately is "to find healthy ways to relate to your deceased loved one" (Rando, 1988, p. 238), in concurrence with our own view that, despite the loss of the partner, the relationship *does not end* – it rather continues, albeit on a different level (Harvey, et al., 1982).

PERSONAL RESOLUTION

> Mark would sing me a song every night and every morning. We called it the Petunia song. It was a dumb song, really dumb. Mark would make up a different tune and lyrics each time, but it never rhymed, and it was never remotely melodious. . . . Really dumb, but every time Mark sang it, I felt secure and loved in a way I had never dreamed possible. I had always meant to write down some of the words, because they were so silly and funny and made me feel so happy; but I never did. And now I couldn't remember them. I could remember the feeling, but I couldn't really remember the words.
>
> Which was not the worst way to begin to forget.
>
> (Ephron, 1983, pp. 177–8)

The term "griefwork" suggests, aptly, that grief has a job to do. That job includes, among other tasks, "beginning to forget," as Ephron observes, in the conclusion to her fictionalized autobiographical account of her own divorce. But the forgetting agenda is as dialectical as the self-versus-other process of mourning. Grievers want to forget, but they want to remember as well. And it is more complex than selective forgetting, trying to remember the "good times" and forget the "bad." For remembering only the good times would make the loss unbearable, impossible to understand, just as remembering only the bad times invalidates the relationship itself and undermines the reason and worth of the grieving partner. If he was so rotten, why did I stay with him? If it was all bad, why do I feel so lost now that it's over?

Again and again, grievers cite the importance of being able to talk or write to preserve their fragile and elusive relationship memories. A 74-year-old man who had lost both of his brothers in World War II recalled the pain of the loss with a fresh poignancy, and commented on the importance of sharing his memories with others:

> Friends of my brothers helped by discussing their own experiences with my brothers, both good and bad. Got much help from their reminiscences about funny and humorous things they had been involved in with my brothers. Fortunately I have always had a great and very close relation with my wife. It helps that she, too, knew my brothers well and we sometimes yet talk about them.[7]

The widow who was quoted above (p. 89), about the helpfulness of having friends and neighbors gather together to recount memories of her late husband, later pursued her own personal cherishment ritual:

> He died three months before our 40th wedding anniversary and although friends asked me out (we were married on Christmas Day), I chose to spend my anniversary *with him*. I re-read our old love letters and giggled at some of the recollections. I watched reels of movie film of our wedding and honeymoon, and this made me feel good because once again I was able to see him as young and strong and handsome and not as the wasted, sickly person I remembered for the last nine years.

Another woman, whose husband had left her suddenly after 23 years of marriage, expressed conflict about the mixture of pain and pleasure in her recollections, and wondered whether she was remembering more now than she used to:

> I do remember good things about our marriage—some of the funny things, the sweet, thoughtful gestures. I also remember the bad times, but I don't dwell on them. . . . My feelings now are, weren't we lucky to have had so much once. Perhaps now at 67 I'm remembering more often.[8]

In some cases, coping with grief and resuming normal, "everyday" living requires an escape route, a lifestyle or course of action that helps one to forget. A 63-year-old woman recounted how her husband of many years had simply announced that he no longer wished to be married, but wished to spend his remaining years "finding himself" in more solitary pursuits:

> I was devastated when I heard this . . . Our son was to be married in four months . . . [My husband] suggested that we not go "public" with the divorce until after the wedding. I agreed . . . Since we continued to live in the same house for four months I was able to ask him questions and show him how I felt expressing grief, anger, etc. Since we agreed not to tell anyone until after the wedding I was not able to have support from anyone but a counselor.
>   . . . Being in a completely different environment where I am not being continually bombarded with memories of him has helped me immensely . . .[9]

Remembering the lost person is important if the relationship is to be validated, if self-worth is to be retained. But memories come unbidden and bring fresh grief and pain. Asked how best to describe memories of lost love, members of a class of over-60-year-olds chose the term "bittersweet" as most appropriate. Memories are also, by nature, ironic, because they view past musings from the informed perspective of the present, the "future" that the past could only guess at. For example, in the lyrics of Joni Mitchell's song "The Last Time I Saw Richard," the storyteller's reminiscence comes full circle by returning to a painful prophecy. She recalls how, years before, Richard had scoffed at her "romantic" dreams. Predicting that she would end up "cynical and drunk and boring someone in some dark cafe." After a stanza or two lamenting Richard's own rather unromantic life-course, the storyteller acknowledges that she herself has been – just as Richard predicted – recounting her memories to strangers in cafés.

In forming and retailing the account, the griever pulls at the fibers of memory, weaving and re-weaving the strands for various audiences, moods, and motives. Whether the account is written or spoken or not quite subarticulated, it takes shape through its applications as a rich tapestry, depicting scenes from one's relationship life. Sometimes the griever begins the account-making process diffusely, with no clear focus or desire:

> I went to the cemetery where my husband was buried quite often, at first, then it tapered off. I wrote down my feelings. I wrote and wrote and wrote—things I couldn't discuss with others. I talked about my feelings a lot, too.
>   (61-year-old retired teacher)[10]

At other times, one's account-making may begin in a quest for peace of mind, as in assuaging this woman's guilt over her mother's death in a nursing home, where she had placed her three years earlier.

> My cousin and some friends helped – just by calling or visiting me – and we
> *talked* about her and I came to terms with the fact that she had received
> excellent care.[11]

In our grief we may find ourselves seeking to express ideas and
feelings that transcend mundane conversation, and so turn to more
literary structure:

> [My mother] was only 58 . . . when she died of heart disease after several
> months of critical illness. . . She realized she was going to die . . . She said to
> me, "I don't want to die. I should have 20 more years." She died the next day.
> . . . About 15 years after Mom died, I was thinking about her one day, so I
> wrote [a] poem to her . . .
>
> (68-year-old retired teacher)[12]

Ultimately, account-making *begins* within the framework of one's
personal quest for meaning, closure, understanding what happened
and why, or why it "had" to, or what loss means for love, intimacy,
and action. The following excerpts from respondents to our survey
of Elderhostel participants illustrate various forms of this quest:

> I couldn't believe that this was happening to such a good man. It wasn't fair.
> The damn platitudes and fundamental sayings brought my anger to the surface
> in a profane way . . . I wish to God [that] God would let me in on the purpose
> because I sure as hell don't see how or why it has happened to him. . .
>
> (66-year-old wife of Alzheimer's victim)

> He told others he had never loved me. The years we had spent together, what
> meaning did they have? . . . On the whole, I think I am coping well . . . Yet I
> am still trying to figure out what went wrong; still trying to make sense of
> those years we spent together.
>
> (62-year-old divorced librarian)

> The loss of an infant son who died after one day of life . . . was particularly
> painful because of his being our first child. . . . Today the child would have a
> good chance of being saved; this was 1963. This was the hardest thing I have
> had to go through . . . Picking out the clothes he would wear, seeing the
> near-perfect (to me!) features and finally the funeral was a soul-wrenching
> experience. . . . We still think of the event . . . and wonder what our
> 26-year-old son would be like . . .
>
> (68-year-old man, retired instructor)

Account-making in grief is founded in several needs: the preserva-
tion and protection of memory; the translation of feelings and
wishes; the execution of particular motives, like guilt and rationali-

zation; and the achievement of closure. Such is the personal agenda of account-making in grief. But account-making in the wake of relationship loss also serves an important set of social functions.

SOCIAL RESOLUTION

> I did not attend his funeral, but I wrote a nice letter saying I approved it.
>   Mark Twain (used in Winokur, 1987)

What is the role of one's social network – friends, relatives and colleagues – in the wake of loss? Most work on this question has focused on the purported functions and effects of social support (e.g., Lopata, 1988; Vachon and Stylianos, 1988). Initial gestures of support may take the form of frozen platitudes, or of advice, one of the least helpful forms of response to grief (Wortman and Lehman, 1985; Vachon and Stylianos, 1988). There is such a thing as "bad" social support, in that its emptiness or normative pressure may confuse and discourage the griever. However, Rosenblatt (1988) comments:

> it is probably always wrong (although not necessarily always a mistake) to say to another, "I know exactly how you feel." Yet basic human similarity, life experience, and a knowledge of another person's situation can provide enough knowledge about what another person feels to allow empathy and an appreciation of their pain, anger, confusion, and many other emotions. Imperfect knowledge still allows effective listening and supportiveness and appropriately connecting actions (Rosenblatt, 1988, p. 76).

Is there a difference between recording one's feelings and reminiscences in a private diary or meditation, and expressing them to another person? The former is an essentially private process, marked by a neglect of – even a disdain for – intelligible presentation to others. Alice Koller began her own painful and powerful self-analysis with a detailed diary, ultimately published almost fifteen years after the fact (Koller, 1982). It is evident that it was not originally written "for" others' eyes, however, by the numerous references to names and relationships that are not explained "for" the reader, and by private, idiosyncratic patterns of words and punctuation. Expressing one's account to others is a social act as much as a public revelation of a private reality. Vaughan (1986) recounts the pattern she experienced in conducting interviews for her own work on breakups and the "uncoupling" process:

I asked them to tell me about their relationship, beginning with the moment when they first sensed something was wrong. They attempted to put their experience in chronological order, and I interjected questions along the way. People were often painfully candid. . . . As each story unfolded, it seemed to develop a momentum all its own. The telling of it regenerated past emotions that carried the story along . . . At the same time, they demonstrated concern with what I thought by apologizing for tears or anger, or asking me if something they felt or did or thought in the relationship was "normal". (Vaughan, 1986, p. 199)

Platitudes

The word "platitude" derives from a series of Latin and Old French roots meaning "flat," referring to the fact that such expressions are broad, trite, and lacking in originality. Not long ago one of the authors (ALW) met an acquaintance, an older man who had been a student in a class she taught for senior citizens. In conversing to catch up on each other's lives, he told her that he and his wife were struggling with the serious illness of their daughter, an experience whose stress was compounded by the fact that they had always expected that it would be she who would eventually care for them, not vice versa. When the author expressed her sympathy and concern and asked him to keep in touch, he said they wcrc bearing up as best they all could. "The worst part about it all," he confessed, almost laughing, "is all the damn *platitudes* we have had to hear in the last few months!" For the remainder of the conversation the author chose commiserations very carefully, conscious of how many offerings might be cliches.

The author first elaborated on the connection between platitudes and account-making as follows:

I have been thinking about my former student and that conversation again as I write this, and earlier today when I attended the funeral of an old friend. My friend, just my age, and his new wife had both been killed in a car accident in another state. The memorial service hosted a standing-room-only crowd, mostly young adults, all of us caught between the pain of loss and the confusion of denial and disbelief. Many of us in attendance were seeing each other for the first time in months or years, and began the familiar "How *are* you?" and "Long time no see" exchanges, interspersed with whispers of shock and, of course, *platitudes*. From my own lips sprang several along the lines of "Well, I hear they were really happy together," and "I guess it must have been really quick," and "I suppose we're being selfish to be so sad, because we're the ones left behind." Even as I spoke and listened, I thought of my student and his disgust with the unoriginal, pedestrian language of loss. (Author's files).

An expression of sympathy may be "flat" because it is insincere or naive. But it may also be flat, to stretch a metaphor, because it addresses a "level" reality: loss is a great leveler. No one may "know exactly how you feel," but relationship loss is surely one of the basic human experiences, a common denominator of life and intimacy. This may not excuse the fact that many platitudes are unhelpful. But it may explain why they are so platitudinous. There simply may not be very many new, original ways to express our sentiments surrounding experiences so basic and ineffable as loss—and the grief that swells in its wake.

Platitudes and abbreviated expressions of sympathy or helplessness in the face of loss may exemplify what, in chapter 8, we shall refer to as "gists" of accounts. A gist (from *Geist* or spirit) captures the essence of an account – a summary of the story, a capsule version of the range of understandings and emotions associated with intimacy or, in the case of grief, with loss. By definition a gist is brief, spare, unelaborated. But it may be no less apt or touching in its conciseness.

The Language of Loss

When we attempt to express the inexpressible our endeavors come up against the limitations of our words and syntax. The language of loss is contextually complicated by the irony that communication is basically *social*, and yet the experience of loss is essentially *private*. Is there a clearer example of the uses and confusions of social comparison than one observes at a funeral? Each person hopes he or she is behaving appropriately, and each scans the room self-consciously to check and compare movements, postures, and facial expressions. There are at least two agendas – personal grief and social contact – involved in attending a memorial service, and these agendas are as conflictual as they are complementary. Here the most existential issues dissolve into banter and casual conversation. No wonder our language – when we can find words – packages profound insights in platitudes and banalities. What else can we really expect of ourselves or of others? One young woman apologized for her lack of tears at the funeral of her young brother: "I don't know *why* I haven't cried. I'm sorry. I'm *new* at this." (Author's files).

The language of loss is couched in euphemisms – literally, speaking "nothing but good" of the dead (*de mortuis nil nisi bonum*). Instead of expressing our pain or fear, we joke about the excesses of funereal ritual or about the high cost of dying. The deceased has not "died", but rather "departed," "passed on," "passed away," "left us," "expired," or simply "gone." When the loss is distant or scorned, we may employ irreverent idioms like "bit the dust," "bought the farm," and "kicked the bucket" – as if death were a remote improbability for any of us.

The evasiveness of such non-talk is characteristic of denial, the earliest common reaction to the reality of death (Kubler-Ross, 1969). But the very profusion of platitudes contradicts the appeal of denial; the simplest system of denial would surely be to maintain silence. But this is not feasible since grief has a *social* agenda as well as a personal one. We *will* see and interact with others, in addition to our own intensely private memories, reflections, and pain. This dialectic between introspection and exchange accounts for much of the irony, frustration, and even the humor of the language of loss. In our grief we have "work" to do: we must confront our own fear and pain surrounding the loss and its reminder of our own fragility and mortality. And we must forge a new social identity and network with those who remain, along with us, left behind by those who have "gone."

USING ACCOUNTS IN GRIEF WORK

> Loss is inescapable. Deaths, estrangements, and separations are part of life. Recoveries tend to be either more or less adequate; only rarely can they be said to be either complete or entirely absent. Most of us have character structures influenced by partial recovery from loss. . . . Loss and pain are inescapable, but permanent damage should not be. (Weiss 1988, pp. 50–1)

Shortly after beginning to write this chapter, the author whose old friend was killed in an automobile accident received a letter from a close friend who was the former girlfriend of the accident victim. The letter was a thank-you for expressions of sympathy and grief over the loss, but she went beyond those sentiments:

> Grief, yes, I was certainly suffering from the grief of Tony's death. Even as I write these words I do not believe it fully. . . . You all know very well how close Tony and I were for so so many years. We dated for four years, then off and on for two more. He made several quiet trips to Chicago to see me [after I had moved here]. We made our peace from lovers to friends years ago. And close friends we were indeed. He knew me before I even went to college. I was 18 and he was 24. He helped me grow up, showed me the world, gave me worth and dignity when I was a shy, [provincial] girl with little idea of self

worth and no sophistication whatsoever. He taught me love, worth, and helped me grow up gently and wisely. He was my first love and my first friend from outside my narrow little [hometown]. He accepted me fully before I even accepted my own background. Tony was Tony. Sweet, constant, cheerful and a friend to all. We were terribly in love for a very, very long time.[13]

How naturally this *story* emerges from expressions of grief, disbelief, and commiseration! In expressing our grief we seem to feel compelled to list our "credentials" in mourning: here is why *I* am grief-stricken, this is what *I* once had or knew – and now have lost. Multiply this validation exercise by several friends and relatives, and grief is a *social* experience every bit as much as it is a personal one. Anyone who has attended a crowded funeral or memorial service (or court case or wedding or graduation ceremony, to balance the light-hearted with the lugubrious) has had the experience of looking about oneself and wondering "Who is *that*? How does (or did) he or she know the bride/graduate/deceased?" This is also usually an acceptable line of introduction. We may approach the stranger after the formal ceremony and ask, "How are you connected with these proceedings?" Others can ask us the same. We may complain or feel uneasy about the fact that we "don't know how to behave" at these rare landmark occasions – as if others in attendance did this all the time – and find our conversational leads oddly colloquial at such an unordinary event. People at funerals smile and raise their eyebrows in greeting familiar faces across the chapel, and approach each other in the parking lot with "How *are* you?" Thus begin our conversations, our reconnections with safe banality. And what do we talk about, what do we tell? Our stories, as often as not. Our accounts of what we are doing here, what we remember, and why we "belong."

People who share memories and accounts of relationships with mutual friends will discover two dimensions of comparison: how much their accounts converge, and how much they diverge. The convergence is socially reassuring; I obviously knew him or her as well as you did, I have similar memories. The divergence can be self-servingly satisfying: I have experienced this person in a way that no one else has; no one else possesses these memories or stakes this claim. If accounts are thus to function as a sort of social glue *and* self-validation, they must be *related*. People have to share them, offer them, cite them, listen to them, confirm them. Accounts become our social credentials only in the process and the fact of our exchanging them. They are the currency of our shared history and continued affilation. They prove, "I was here. I knew this person. And now I am different."

THERAPEUTIC ACCOUNT-MAKING

> They talked about their fear as if talking about it would make the images go
> away.
>> (CBS News reporter Betsy Aaron, on the survivors of the crash of
>> United Airlines Flight 232 in Sioux City, Iowa, in July 1989)

Is account-making a compulsion? Surely not everyone is as articulate or verbal as the subjects and authors we are citing here. But could the process of formulating one's story be a matter of urgency rather than deliberation? Reporters find no shortage of survivors willing to talk in the wake of a tragedy. Who is doing whom the favor?

If account-making is prompted by personal needs and social roles, can it be engineered to useful effect – or must it be spontaneous to be helpful? A number of grief theorists and psychotherapists think not. They recommend, for those acutely suffering the incapacitation of blinding grief, a strategic, methodical program of grieving prior to re-emerging (the swimming metaphor again) into "normal" (albeit altered) living. Most such programs of structured grieving include a stage or ongoing process of account-making. For example, one grief consultant cautions the newly bereaved to prepare for the need to "memorialize" the deceased person in some personally meaningful way (Staudacher, 1987). The obvious standard for such a process is a memorial *service* or ceremony, usually public and attended by others. But less ritualistic forms include talking about the deceased person, or recording others' talk. It can take shape according to the griever's talents and drives, as a young actor recounts:

> After my father's death, I wrote a play, a one-man show about his life, his
> thoughts, his dreams and my relationship to him. I performed it in local
> theater and then was invited to perform it at theater festivals abroad. It was
> my tribute to his life (Staudacher, 1987, p. 93).

Staudacher further warns that such verbal memorials are not likely to be a "one-shot deal"; the story will be repeated, again and again, and the accepting listener must be prepared for what may seem like an endless-loop replay of the griever's memories:

> Every time you talk about it, every time you go through your story and talk
> about some part of the grief process, as painful as it might be at the moment, it

becomes easier. Some people need to continue to talk about it a few times. Some people need to continue to talk about it over and over again. I felt the need for a long time to tell the story. At least a year.

(Survivor of a neonatal death and a support group facilitator, in Staudacher, 1987, p. 227)

Such recycling is characteristic of what Weiss (1975) has called "obsessive review" in the wake of relationship termination: the newly separated individual examines her memory relentlessly, searching for clues that will help to explain why and how this could have happened.

What aspects of account-making and account-relating are specifically therapeutic? Staudacher argues that, minimally, expressing one's feelings about the loss is essential to healing. Self-expression may afford the griever a rare opportunity to listen to her own feelings:

I thought I knew how to handle it. I knew I was going to go through anger. I knew I was going to go through periods of being vulnerable. Even though I intellectualized it, I still had to go through it and experience it. I made myself sick physically because I wasn't letting my feelings out.

(Widow whose 42–year-old husband died suddenly of a heart attack, in Staudacher, 1987, p. 60)

Listeners can be more validating than soliloquy, but not just any listener will do, as this male survivor complains:

I can talk to my sister about the macho thing and a woman can be very understanding, very sympathetic, but it doesn't mean a hell of a lot unless it comes from a man

(Staudacher, 1987, p. 61)

And if talking will not do it, or is not enough, Staudacher counsels the griever to write: write about your strongest feelings in your grief; write a valediction to the lost individual; write a description of him or her as only you could perceive and express.

Do talking and writing about the loss help? There is little direct research confirmation of this (as we discuss in developing our model of account-making in response to stress), but an abundance of supportive common sense and folk wisdom. One can also find impassioned testimony that *not* talking is *un*helpful – even dangerously unhealthy. News articles addressing the tragedy of suicide often note the compounding of grief by feeling unable to talk openly about the loss. In one such interview (Svetvilas, 1989), a woman whose friend had committed suicide years earlier found her own grieving still complicated by his family's persistent denial that he had killed himself Not only had all the family members been more adversely affected by such denial, but the friend found herself alone and isolated when no one else would acknowledge the suicide.

Failure to grieve in a timely and focused manner may develop into a psychological disorder, sooner or later. The novelist William Styron claims that his own near-suicidal depression had such origins, attributing it to an "incomplete mourning" experience suffered after his own mother's death when he was 13, and suggesting to one reviewer that he "dealt with" this depression in his novels long before he experienced it consciously (Romine, 1989).

Talking or writing about one's feelings also moves one toward closure. One aspect of grief is often guilt or anger over "unfinished business" with the deceased or absent person. In developing and relating her account, the griever may hear herself come up with new hypotheses and insights, guesses about how conflicts might have been resolved, fantasies about "happily-ever-afters" that were prematurely ended. For those who are unable to develop such conclusions or speculations on their own, Tatelbaum (1980) advises undertaking Gestalt therapy as a more direct way of "finishing" the unfinished business. One such technique involves speaking to the "empty chair" as if it contained the lost person, and saying what one has wished to say. This is surprisingly difficult and not necessarily less emotional than a flesh-and-blood confrontation. The griever completes the "dialogue" by taking the chair herself and responding to her own questions and assertions, from the perspective of the unavailable partner. The goal is obviously not a real negotiation, since there is only one live party to this "interaction," but rather accessing one's deeper, unarticulated feelings about the loss and its repercussions.

Other writers and counselors are beginning to develop programs and techniques for dealing with loss. Kingma (1987) recommends keeping a "personal workbook" to facilitate dealing with the break-up of a close relationship. The workbook should be composed of written exercises that are part of what she calls "rituals for parting." The first such exercise involves "Telling the Love Story" – including the "clue of failure," the fatal flaw in the relationship that would later prove its undoing. In contrast, the second exercise involves "Telling the Real Story," including one's own real agenda and "developmental task," one's best guess about the partner's motives and agenda. Kingma further suggests:

> If the story of your relationship [were] written up as a novel or made into a movie, what would it be called? Some examples: *Great Expectations*; *Two Ships That Should Have Passed in the Night*; *The Year of Living Dangerously*; *More is Less*; *Too Many Gin and Tonics* (Kingma, 1987, p 111)

Kingma recommends supplementary exercises like writing letters (that will never be sent) expressing one's feelings and ticking off one's justifications. All in all, Kingma's therapeutic program would be well met by developing a thorough account. We argue that account-making develops "naturally" in response to relationship trauma; Kingma suggests it can be undertaken consciously and deliberately to expedite grief and recovery.

The paradox of long-term grief, according to Rando (1988), is that the griever must find a way to develop a "new relationship" with the loved one – who is unavailable physically and/or symbolically. How is this to be accomplished? Rando recommends a variety of strategies and activities, ranging from maintaining habits or commitments originally begun by the lost person to allowing oneself repeatedly "to cry and cry, talk and talk, review and review without the interruption of anyone else's sanity" (Rando, 1988, p. 248). Rando advises:

> You will have to repeatedly review the entire relationship, back to its earliest beginnings and all the hopes and fantasies that formed it. You will need to discuss its ups and downs, its course and development, its crises and joys – all aspects of it through the years. . . This is how you slowly begin to withdraw your emotional energy from your loved one and reestablish a new relationship with him that is not based on the give-and-take of life (Rando, 1988, p. 250)

Accounts have pedagogical value as well as emotional therapeutic value. Greenberg and Greenberg (1979) encourage Jewish parents and teachers to tell children stories about the Holocaust, especially from personal perspectives and memories:

> [An] important factor in our children's understanding of the Holocaust has been our friendship with many survivors. The Holocaust does not automatically come up in our conversations together. In fact, many survivors feel that no one wants to hear about the Holocaust and are reluctant to discuss their experiences. . . At times, our children have seen us, our eyes glistening, in quiet conversation with our friends. Sometimes they would overhear; sometimes they would ask later; sometimes we offered without their asking. We have always told them the tales we felt they could bear to hear (Greenberg and Greenberg, 1979, p. 280).

Finally, we must acknowledge that, in account-making as part of grief, the griever may have an ongoing or occasional agenda of addressing the lost person directly, though impossibly. When we relate our accounts to living others, we may force our words into the conventions of third-person narrative: "He could always make me laugh" or "She had a calming way of reassuring me that everything was going to be all right." But when accounts burst into other forms, as when grievers feel moved to try their unsteady hands at poetry, it seems largely to be addressed *to* deceased or departed individual. The Elderhostel respondent cited earlier wrote a poem *to* her mother, not merely *about* her, and began it thus:

> Oh Mom, I wish that you could be
> My friend, who's just the age of me.

A perusal of almost *any* American newspaper's obituary page will reveal many amateur *In Memoriam* offerings along the same lines: "It was just one year ago today,/the Lord took you another way . . ." These are not eulogies; they are entreaties, one-sided dialogues, conversations continued beyond an interruption.

Writer Linda Hasselstrom, whose recent work is itself an *account* of her life as a woman rancher on the Northern Plains of the United States, has dedicated her book to her late husband, who died of cancer. She opens her journal with a poem addressed "to George," and noting that he has left her, "too fast for me to follow," so that her life has changed completely, and he can continue in her life only "inside" her heart and her memories (Hassetstrom, 1989).

Account-making thus develops in response to loss, in the course of grieving. It encompasses and helps to express emotions like fear, anger, and painful sorrow. It preserves memories and pursues closure and understanding. Our accounts comprise both personal resolution and social restructuring. They chronicle our relationships, and may even attempt to continue them beyond cold barriers. In grief, then, we can see account-making in all of its roles and dynamics, giving form and even timelessness to the very human search for answers.

SUMMARY

Account-making may play an important part in the process of grieving. Grief work involves completing several tasks, any of which might be facilitated or eased in the course of remembering. composing, and sharing one's account of the new-lost relationship. Account-making may follow the stages of grief, involving feelings, thoughts, and language that first avoid the loss, then confront it, and finally establish the grievers's identity in a new life without the lost person. Grief work, and the role of accounts therein, may have two tasks: a personal agenda of grief and coping; and a social program focused on sharing stories with others. Glimmers of the account may surface in sudden grief spasms and triggered memories and associations. They may also be resurrected as the griever deliberately attempts to reconstruct remembrances and memorials of a deceased loved one. Many grief rituals appear to be structured to encourage social contact and account-sharing. Examples have been provided of the importance to grievers of being able to share and exchange feelings and memories with others. Examples have also been provided of the ways in which grievers may use accounts to preserve and refine their memories of past relationships, and develop new identities and social roles. Finally, account-making can be important both in informal, personal resolution of grief and in more formal therapeutic strategy to assist those who are bereaved.

6 An Evolutionary Perspective on Account-making

It began in what seemed in my personal narratizations as an individual choice of a problem with which I have had an intense involvement for most of my life: the problem of the nature and origin of all this invisible country of touchless rememberings and unshowable reveries, this introcosm that is more myself than anything I can find in any mirror . . .

Julian Jaynes, 1976

There exists . . . a recent development, deeply involved with the evolution of consciousness, which is full of promise; and this is the growth of the sense of the past in our minds.

John Lukacs, 1970

The present chapter will present a quite speculative analysis regarding the evolutionary stature and significance of account-making in the human species. In this analysis, we shall rely considerably upon Jaynes' *The Origins of Consciousness in the Breakdown of the Bicameral Mind* (1976). In this influential book, Jaynes, a psychologist, argues for and traces archaeological evidence suggesting that ancient peoples did not "think" as humans do today. Those peoples who lived in periods over 3,000 years ago it is argued did not introspect. Rather, they experienced auditory hallucinations – voices of gods actually heard, as in the Old Testament or the *Iliad*. Such voices, Jaynes contends, came from the brain's right hemisphere and told a person what to do in circumstances of stress or vulnerability. This mentality of these ancient peoples is called the 'bicameral mind.' As Jaynes says,

> The preposterous hypothesis we have come to . . . is that at one time human nature was split in two, an executive part called a god, and a follower part called a man. Neither part was conscious. This is almost incomprehensible to us. And since we are conscious, and wish to understand, we wish to reduce this to something familiar in our experience . . . (Jaynes, 1976, p. 84)

Jaynes argues at great length that catastrophe and cataclysm in the earth's environment forced ancient peoples to *learn consciousness* and hence become dominated by the left hemisphere of the brain. Overall, Jaynes examines three forms of human awareness: the bicameral or god-run mind; the modern or problem-solving mind; and contemporary throw-backs to bicamerality, such as hypnosis, schizophrenia, and poetic and religious zeal and frenzied behavior. As the reviewers of Jaynes' striking thesis proclaimed, no previous scholar of the human condition has proposed a theory so bold and encompassing.

ACCOUNT-MAKING AND LEFT-BRAIN DOMINANCE

The principal feature of the human who came on the scene around 3,000 years ago in Jaynes' theory is that of consciousness, the ability to reflect about self, others, time – the past, present, future – and even one's own death. Where does account-making enter the picture in the evolution of consciousness? It enters when the "I" is developed. Interestingly, for both Jaynes and the father of symbolic interactionism George Herbert Mead (1934), the "I" represents the human's sense of awareness. To Jaynes, the "I" is capable of logical reasoning about behavior, of trying to explain events in one's life and the environment, of giving verbal answers to questions that arise in one's own inner mental life. It is the quality we most often think of (though we have different terms for it) when we try to reduce the concept of human to its core essence. Mead viewed the "I" as the reflexive agent of socialization:

> The "I" . . . never can exist as an object in consciousness, but the very conversational character of our inner experience, the very process of replying to one's own talk, implies an "I" behind the scenes who answers to the gestures, the symbols, that arise in consciousness. The "I" is the transcendental self of Kant, the soul that James conceived behind the scene holding on to the skirts of an idea to give it an added increment of emphasis. (Mead, 1934, p. 141)

Thus, while these two theorists have somewhat different views of the "I", this entity or process may be viewed as the prime mover in left-dominant mental activity, in the socialized human's taking the role of others as symbolic interactional activity, and as the account-maker trying to find meaning and make sense out of events in his or her life.

In his treatment of schizophrenia as a modern form of the bicameral condition, Jaynes develops the "I" concept further:

> The whole idea that a person can explain himself, something which in the bicameral era was distinctly the function of gods, can no longer occur . . . . With the loss of the analog "I," its mind-space, and the ability to narratize, behavior is either responding to hallucinated directions, or continues on by habit. The remnant of the self feels like a commanded automation, as if someone else were moving the body about. (Jaynes, 1976, p. 421)

Our thesis is that the account is the product of the "I", and account-making is the same activity as this narratization process that Jaynes mentions in arguing that people suffering from schizophrenia cannot perform narratization. Account-making would appear to be one of the most representative activities of left-brain functioning. In account-making, the human seeks to justify actions, construe purpose and meaning, and more generally learn, adapt, and survive. Over an extended period of time, the chief mission of the account is not the survival of the individual, but rather the survival of the species and its culture and civilization. We as reflective individuals learn that our personal death is a certainty – a matter of some gloom to most. Thus, the account serves to provide a sense of immortality to us as beings cognizant of our own relatively imminent demise. In the context of eons of time, the account-making activity and its very continuity make our personal death seem more bearable. Accounts provide a bridge across time and history. In accounts, we leave for our successors some legacy of beliefs, values, traditions, depictions of precious moments and of strong emotions such as love – we leave "our good name" and all that signifies in terms of understanding the world.

Another part of our thesis is that the demand for account-making skill and perceived need for its development is increasing over time under left-brain dominance. As our earlier analysis of account-making and stress suggests, the human species is incurring heavy account-making demands as the pace and complexity of modern life intensify. Cultural advance becomes more and more defined in terms of our account-making sophistication, whether in astrophysics or the study of close relationships. A significant cultural development of the 1970s and 80s in the domain of close relationships involves the human male's increased acceptance of emotional expressiveness, and "relationship talk" in general, as a positive male attribute (Rubin, 1983). Enhanced skill at account-making, and a greater devotion to this activity, would appear to be positively correlated with a number or cultural events, including more sophisticated technology, greater travel opportunities and mobility, more leisure-time, and an increased number of friends, partners, and/or lovers over the course of life for many people in this world. Also, as implied in chapters 2 and 3, the increased attention to accounts by the ordinary person comes from the fact that alongside this pace of living are personal traumas and psychological hurt from disappointments in love, work, and central quests in one's life. The information overload on the mind created by living in such a social psychological milieu can be addressed only via a type of cognitive organization which the account well represents. It tidies up otherwise unbearably complex, disjointed, stupefying, and even terrifying details and minutiae. From discrete pieces of data, it derives coherence and apparent direction. Together with the historical function noted above, the account provides the vehicle for generation after generation to discern meaningful threads in their/our existence.

Consistent with Jaynes' reasoning, two physiological psychologists, Gazzaniga and Le Doux (1978), have summarized the careful investigation of the behaviour of patients whose left and right brain hemispheres have been surgically separated. They conclude that, in most people, the left hemisphere contains the material and functioning that make us feel like single, purposeful beings – that is, our language system: "It is as if the verbal self looks out and sees what the person is doing, and from that knowledge it interprets reality" (Gazzaniga and Le Doux, 1978, p. 150).

BRAIN DOMINANCE, LOVE, AND ACCOUNTS

In an analysis of two psychologies of love, McClelland (1986) posits an interesting role of left and right brain functioning in love processes, which has implication for account-making. According to McClelland, one type of love that is theorized by many scholars involves an emphasis on the reasons for love, especially the benefits that people obtain in love relationships, such as confiding in the other person, sexuality, and help with one's career (e.g. Walster,

Walster, and Berscheid, 1978; Berscheid, 1983; Kelley et al., 1983). On the other hand, McClelland contends that another type of love is conceived by other scholars which focuses on the experiences people have when they are in love (e.g. McAdams, 1980, 1982). McClelland notes that these scholars use different measures to investigate these different views of love and that the latter view of love (namely, the type represented in McAdams' work) is found particularly in the writing and theoretical work of poets, clinicians, and physiological psychologists. He suggests that this approach to love, emphasizing its basic felt experience, characterizes right-brain functioning, while the former approach, emphasizing conscious evaluation and attribution, characterizes left-brain functioning. McClelland also argues that his own work on fantasy and imaginative experiences (using projective techniques including the Thematic Apperception Test) supports the right hemispheric view and that, overall, this differentiation between left-brain reports of love and right-brain experience of love better predicts affiliative behavior.

Our own analysis of account-making is consistent with McClelland's ideas about the left hemisphere's role in making judgements and attributions. Although we also argue that account-making involves emotional processes to a considerable degree (see chapter 3), none the less the account is mainly a product of the intellect and of conscious reasoning about cause and effect and the association of events.

THE CENTRALITY OF CONTROL MOTIVATION

Returning to one of the primary motivations for account-making, virtually the whole of left-brain-driven problem-solving and attributional activity may be seen as serving the human's need to feel personal control in managing one's own life and in being able to have some predictability in one's environment. A major strand of work in social psychology over the last two decades has centered on the role of perceived control in facilitating various forms of social behavior and social interaction (Wortman, 1975; Seligman, 1975). Presumably, the feeling of control enhances performance and satisfaction (Langer and Rodin, 1976). Evidence also suggests that feelings of personal freedom of choice and responsibility are correlated with perceived control in a situation (Harvey, Harris, and Barnes, 1975; Harvey, Harris, and Lightner, 1979). As Thompson (1981) contends, control "does not even have to be real, *just perceived*, for it to have effects" (p. 89, emphasis added). Although we know of no direct evidence on this hypothesis, quantity and quality of account-making, a prime intellectual-emotional activity, should be strongly and positively correlated with the feelings of control, freedom, and responsibility across many settings. We assume that people form what has been referred to as a sense of "retrospective control" (Thompson, 1981) through the process of looking back and analyzing causality associated with past events (i.e. account-making when extended to the form of story-like constructions). They then bring that sense of attained control to new situations. They also bring to new situations habits and beliefs about the value (or lack thereof) of continuing to probe the causal and other elements underlying events in their lives. We believe that all of this activity epitomizes left-hemisphere functioning as described in Jaynes' (1976) theory.

It is interesting to consider that, as implied in chapter 5, a powerful step in the healthy grieving process is that of "letting go." Such a step helps one accept the death of a close other and it also permits a person to take the final step in relaxing control prior to one's own death. This activity emphasizes letting nature take its course and may be assumed to be primarily under the jurisdiction of the right brain. A major conclusion of Jaynes' (1976) book is that we as modern people have moved so far away from our ancient ancestors' adherence to right-brain emphasis that we are now driven incessantly onward toward greater attempts to understand and control and, concomitantly, have increasingly encountered uncertainty and foreboding about out future as individuals and as a species. In regard to this departure from our previous bicameral state:

> The learnings that make up a subjective consciousness are powerful and never totally suppressed. And thus the terror and the fury, the agony and the despair. The anxiety attendant upon so cataclysmic a change, the dissonance with the habitual structure of interpersonal relations, and the lack of cultural support and definition for the voices, making them inadequate guides for everyday living, the need to defend against a broken dam of environmental sensory stimulation is flooding all before it – produce a social withdrawal that is a far different thing from the behavior of the *absolutely* social individual of bicameral societies. The conscious man is constantly using his introspection to find "himself" and to know where he is, relevant to his purposes and situation. (Jaynes, 1976, p. 432).

In such a condition, Jaynes suggests that it is no wonder that schizophrenia, chronic depression, and other serious mental disorders are ever expanding in our contemporary world.

LINKAGES TO OTHER IDEAS AND LITERATURES

As may be deduced from our review in chapter 2, there are many examples of contemporary work that may be conceived as representative of theory and research on left-brain dominance. These works derive from many fields and certainly include the work of many cognitive social psychologists. Some further examples embodying implications for the accounts topic include the following.

Planning

A new line of work by Berger and his colleagues emphasizes planning, affect, and social-action generation (Berger, 1988; Berger and Bell, 1988). These researchers assume that complex plans guide and structure social communication and interaction in general. As an illustration of their work, it was found that people with more complex plans for asking others out on a date showed lower levels of nervousness when placed in an interaction in which their goal was to ask another person for a date. This work follows the important contribution of Miller, Galanter, and Pribram's (1960) argument which emphasized the role of plans in structuring behavior. Berger and associates' work also relates to the research (described in chapter 2) of Cody and McLaughlin (e.g. Cody and McLaughlin, in press), by suggesting that strategic interaction and justification-type behavior often involves a planning component.

Schemata

Over the last decade and a half, approaches emphasizing cognitive schemata constructs have dominated in social psychology (Fiske and Taylor, 1984). These approaches, collectively forming the area of social cognition, have branched away from earlier social perception-attribution work in their focus on more molecular cognitive processes and limitations. According to Neisser (1976), a schema is a structure "internal to the perceiver, modifiable by experience, and somehow specific to what is being perceived. The schema accepts the information as it becomes available and is changed by the information; it directs movements and exploratory activities that make more information available by which it is further modified" (Neisser, 1976, p. 554). Presumably, people have schemata about all sorts of objects, most notably including self (Markus, 1977). An example of a self-schema might be: "Last night I spent three hours with a boring guy because I do not have the guts to tell men right off the bat that I am not interested in them." As was suggested in chapter 4, self-schemata are often formed in social interaction and reflect self-fulfillment processes in which people form sets about a target other, act toward the target in line with those schemata, and influence the target to adopt similar schemata about self and act consistent with such schemata (Snyder and Swann, 1978; Darley and Fazio, 1980).

Information and Influence

Richard Petty and John Cacioppo are two of the leading scholars in social psychology in articulating how attitudes are influenced by cognitive processes (e.g. Petty and Cacioppo, 1986). In their well-regarded theory of persuasion, referred to as the Elaboration Likelihood Model, Petty and Cacioppo argue and provide data to support the view that there are two routes to persuasion. The *peripheral* route is subject to the effect of cues in the attitude change situation such as the expertise or attractiveness of the communicator. In contrast, the *central* route involves a cognitive elaboration process by the recipient of message content. This model assumes that the recipient who is being influenced by central route activity will engage in a high level of careful examination of the pros and cons of messages (and degrees of counterarguing). We believe that this central processing activity in persuasion setting may often be subsumed by more general account-making activity. For example, a person may develop an account about an interaction with an acquaintance who is trying to influence him or her to move the relationship toward greater intimacy. The account may involve considerable central-route processing and various projections and attributions of motive to the acquaintance.

Similarly, Cacioppo and Petty (1982) have proposed that some people have a greater need for cognition than do others. They have developed and validated a scale to assess need for cognition and linked this trait to various cognitive and social activities. In this conception, the person high in need for cognition has a relatively strong inclination to engage in effortful causal analysis. We would predict that the person high in need for cognition is likely to engage in more in-depth account-making, and possibly simply a higher *quantity* of account-making, than does the person low in need for cognition.

Cognition and Coping

The Summer 1989 issue of *Social Cognition*, edited by Leslie Clark, published a set of illustrative works emphasizing what we are referring to as left hemisphere dominant activity. This issue concerns the interface of social cognition and stress and coping. Not only does it exemplify the major stature of theories embracing cognitive models in contemporary social psychology, it also indicates how popular and successful cognitive ideas have become to practitioners in the psychotherapy and medical communities in dealing with stress-related disorders. A paper by Taylor and Schneider (1989) in this special issue represents well this domain of investigation. These investigators propose a cognitive theory of coping that centers on the mental simulation of past, future, and hypothetical events. Simulation may include rehearsals of likely future events, and reconstructions of past events, fantasies, and mixtures of imagined real and hypothetical events. Taylor and Schneider suggest and review evidence to support the argument that event simulation serves both problem-solving and emotional regulation functions for ongoing and past stressors because: (1) simulation increases the perceived truth of the imagined experience; (2) it provides a framework for organizing experience; and (3) it provides a mechanisms for mustering particular emotions and arousal. This conception definitely warrants further empirical test. It resonates well with contemporary work on attribution by Wells and his colleagues suggesting that imagined alternatives to reality are used in assessing the causal role of a past event on an outcome (e.g. Wells and Gavanski, 1988). For example, if a heart attack victim's spouse could have performed cardio-pulmonary resuscitation but did not, the spouse would probably receive a large portion of attributed responsibility should the victim die. Thus, Wells and associates contend, the imagined alternative or simulation heuristic may represent a shortcut for estimating the causality of an event.

In conclusion, these illustrative cognitive and social-cognitive concepts may be conceived as operating within the framework of specific and more general account-making in a person's life. As an illustration, a person's account about a previous disappointment in love may embody plans for the future based on schemata about self, simulations of future possibilities, and degrees of central processing of input (some being persuasion messages) from close others about the account.

MYTHS AND FAMILY STORIES

> Life lives by killing and eating itself,
> casting off death and being reborn.
> Gold and ivory plaque, 720 BC, Baghdad Museum: Campbell, 1988, p. 44

Myths

The lines on the plaque are part of a myth. In this final section, we wish to relate myths and family stories to one another and to accounts, and suggest how each stands at the balance between account-making as a left- or right-brain dominant activity. According to Joseph Campbell (1988), myths may be defined as cultural stories that harmonize individuals' lives within larger frameworks of meaning. He suggested that they pertain not only to the ultraordinary events for which the ancient Greeks created gods (recall our chapter 2 discussion of Bruner's ideas about why stories are told), but also for the more ordinary and troubling events of our lives. He said, "They are the world's dreams. They are archetypal dreams and deal with great human problems" (p. 15). The lines on the plaque at the Baghdad Museum (quote above) probably have a non-obvious meaning connected with the play of nature to create, maintain, and then destroy in an endless cycle (insight provided the authors by Gail Garwood). But more directly, they speak to what Campbell discusses in suggesting that primitive humans developed myths and rituals in order not to feel guilt in killing animals for food. As he said, "These early myths help the psyche to participate without a sense of guilt or fright in the necessary act of life" (Campbell, 1988, p. 73). These early rituals were acts designed in part to appease the animal gods who, if not assuaged, would not reappear, and the hunter would strave to death.

Thus, from this view, myths help fulfil needs. The recognitionof the fact of death and even the need for death represent matters with which societies and humans often have to come to grips. As John Updike says, "The world needed death. It needed death exactly as much as it needed life" ("Killing," in *Trust Me*, 1987, p. 20). Weisman (1984) refers to this need as that of "thanatologic realization." It is an appreciation that death brings every other subcycle of living to its natural conclusion. Weisman suggests that such a realization "signifies how subcycles are woven together, spun out over years, and now snipped away, just as the Fates intended all along" (Weisman, 1984, p. 133).

Campbell emphasized functions of myths that cohere well with what might be viewed as a right hemispheric orientation on the part of the myth-maker and myth-recipient. He suggested that myths help people put their minds in touch with the experience of being alive (cf. earlier discussion of one type of love in McClelland's scheme, pp. 108–9). Campbell makes this point about the difference in studying myths verus the curriculum in most universities:

> They're [myths] stories about the wisdom of life, they really are. What we're learning in our schools is not the wisdom of life. We're learning technologies, we're getting information. There's a curious reluctance on the part of faculties to indicate the life values of their subjects. In our sciences today – and this includes anthropology, linguistics, the study of religions, and so forth – there is a tendency to specialization. And when you know how much a specialist scholar has to know in order to be a competent specialist, you can understand this tendency. (Campbell, 1988, p. 9)

Campbell also suggested that the types of precious moments in memory and understanding, which we discussed especially in chapter 3, often contain the powerful energy from which myths derive. He said, "In the experience of my mother and father who are gone, of whom I was born, I have come to understand that there is more than what was our temporal relationship. Of course there were certain moments in that relationship when an emphatic demonstration of what the relationship was would be brought to my realization. I clearly remember some of those. They stand out as moments of epiphany, or revelation, of the radiance" (ibid., p. 231).

Family Stories

In no sense can the foregoing discussion of myths be adequate to the richness of the topic. (We shall return to Campbell's ideas in chapter 7.) Our purpose in presenting some of Campbell's ideas is that myths represent long-standing stories, which inhere in cultures, and, as such, appear to bear similarity to the products of right hemispheric activity, as discussed by Jaynes (1976). Myths also seem to represent a primitive account-making that may be compared to the modern form of family stories, which in recent years have gained a widespread attention among journalists and writers. Such stories are oral or written narratives about events and characteristics of families that usually are passed down from generation to generation by the elders in a family. For example, a type of family story might tell how the grandparents on one side of a family succeeded in migrating by covered wagon to the western United States during the nineteenth century despite many harsh conditions of travel and the loss of life during the journey.

Keen (1988) discussed family stories and their relationship to cultural myths. In his view, the basic ingredient is the human as story-teller: "We tell stories – myths – about who we are, where we come from, where we are going and how we should live. And the myths we tell become who we are and what we believe – as individuals, families, whole cultures" (1988, p. 44). Like the master account, the family story or myth (it is partly mythical if the true facts are long forgotten, but what remains are the reconstructions of reality) lies mostly submerged beneath the iceberg of individual, familial, or cultural consciousness: outsiders cannot readily disern its varied contents and scope. Keen suggests that family myths may be motivating, just as accounts are. For example, the family myth of the Kennedy clan may inspire others, as well as its own members, to strive for excellence and help us endure hardship and tragedy. Or, like the myths of many an alcoholic or abusive family, they may pass a burden of guilt, shame, and failure from generation to generation – as children adopt the traits of their parents. Although myths may be self-fulfilling and deleterious in their effects, Keen believes that they do not have to be damaging and that a considered examination of one's family and cultural myths can enlighten one's life. In this regard, he notes Santayana's famous aphorism: "Those who do not learn from the past are condemned to repeat it." Or, as the historian John Lukacs (1970) suggested, by knowing your past, you may free your mind from a painful load in the present. As noted in chapter 5, Greenberg and Greenberg (1979) adopt this line of reasoning about the importance of family and cultural stories in making a case for why Jewish parents should consider telling their children about the Holocaust.

Twenty years ago Lukacs (1970) lamented the "passing of the modern age", but observed that, despite the "meaninglessness of letters" and literature since World War II, a countervailing element seemed to be emerging that might portend promise of authentic living. This element, according to Lukacs, involves "the slowly rising consciousness of the meaningfulness of the past, which may create a new appetite for a kind of literature that is engaged in imaginative reconstruction of things that we have once known" (Lukacs, 1970, p. 124).

The past indeed seems "fashionable," evident from even a cursory look at the influence of past decades – or centuries – on clothing styles, popular music, and the visual arts. What distinguishes family stories from a more general nostalgia or affection for days gone by is their unique relevance and implied promise for the recipient (usually the listener) of the story. In her work *Black Sheep and Kissing Cousins*, Elizabeth Stone (1988) explains how she was prompted to collect and analyze family stories in part because of her own fascination with stories she had heard about the girlhood and early adventures of her grandmother. Although the character of her grandmother as portrayed in these stories might not have been particularly grandiose or fantastic, her grandmother had more personal power for her as a figure in a story, because, as Stone asserts: "She wasn't distant like a film star or imaginary like a fairy-tale heroine. She was real. And she was my relative" (1988, p. 4). Family stories have a basis in reality, and thus they hold the power of relevance – personal truth – for the recipient.

Family stories may be viewed in some ways as special forms of accounts, which function in part to bind family members together in a "community of memory" (Bellah et al., 1985). It is not only the content of the family story that holds the attention of recipients; it is the very *process* of its telling – and retelling, again and again – that unifies family members, characterizes their gatherings, and combines entertainment with affection and familiarity. Family stories have other account-like qualities as well. Stone (1988) cites examples of the family stories she heard from her respondents, and their own reactions to them, illustrating some of these qualities. Family stories, like accounts, may be told to explain or defend personal traits or quirks. For example, Stone cites several interviewees as recalling family stories about their own babyhood and growing up, stories that were told to "explain" – or predict – their traits or habits in adulthood. This conforms with our conclusion, reviewed in chapter 4, that accounts have implications for the likability of the account-maker.

Just as accounts may first be formulated in response to trauma or other stressors (see chapter 3), the telling of a family story may be prompted by the need to explain a pattern of family trouble. Stone observes how many of her own family's stories focused on concerns about whether mental illness ran in her family:

> My Aunt Naomi was not the only troubled member of that family. My father was an unstable and unhappy man . . . . Another member of his family, in my generation, also had to be hospitalized for mental illness. What was going on here? Was it genes? Was it some psychic time bomb long ago planted on Ludlow Street? If it was, then I had to worry, too. (1988, p. 97)

In this example, then, the family story, like an account, "works through" family members' concerns about the origins of their problems. The goal would be to identify non-heritable causes – such as a bad marriage or a drinking problem – as the "real" source of difficulty, rather than anything that might inevitably afflict other family members. In other cases, however, it might be that the message of the family story is simply to worry. One of Stone's respondents related a family story about an irresponsible ancestor whose profligacy endangered the family fortune. The family story, oddly, ends without revealing "how it ended," as Stone observes:

> There is no further anecdotal addition where it's made clear that Izzy *did* have his diamonds, stolen, or for that matter, that he didn't. But the fate of the diamonds, says Linda Lefkowitz, is not the point. "The real emotional center of the story," she says, "is that he wasn't alert, he wasn't vigilant. He got seduced and betrayed by gambling and dancing. The story is about worry, which is what they mostly do," an activity which must, to the Lefkowitzes, seem constructive in an otherwise unmanageable world. It is a story whose meaning is clear to those who understand the Lefkowitz worldview. (Stone, 1988, pp. 230–1)

This example also shows that family stories, like accounts, shape perspective and affect one's new identity in the wake of change and tragedy. Some family stories are explicit about the rules to be conveyed in the narrative, as another of Stone's respondents observes: "Being a Medlow means being strong and being tough and being able to survive. Period. It means not having as much as other people. The Medlow family crest, if we had one, would say, 'You'll survive'" (ibid., p. 45).

Finally, like accounts, family stories may conclude with morals, lessons, either subtly woven between the lines or phrased in explicit warnings. In the course of her interviews, Stone observed how one respondent connected two separate story-lines, from different sides of her family, which combined to share a common message – or caveat – about love and marriage:

> "No one ever said this to me in so many words, but there was a message to me: be darn sure about the man you hook up with and don't go for some flash in the pan that attracts you momentarily." She laughs, somewhat abashedly. "I really hadn't thought of it, but this is really very anti-romantic love, isn't it?" (ibid., p. 57)

Stone concludes that we are challenged to make our own meanings out of our many family stories, in order to achieve balance between holding on to our memories and relationships, and letting go of them. Hers is a poignant comment on the paradox that creates the dynamism of accounts in general: the cherishing of one's history, painful and wondrous, in the very process of mourning one's losses.

Family stories reiterate and perpetuate myths about ways to overcome adversity, or promises of family loyalty and endurance, come what may. Like accounts, the power of these myths and promises comes from the baffling depth of the past – not just the past of history and archives, but the past *as* family members *remember* and retell it, for, in Lukacs' words, "the remembered past is what conscious life is all about" (1970, p. 212). The past of accounts or specifically of family stories depends entirely on the account-maker's efforts to compile and retell it.

We would hypothesize that myth-making and, to a degree, family story-telling represent a type of account-making that spans part of the bridge betwen left- and right-brain functioning. The emphasis in these forms of story-telling is somewhat different than was the case for the types of account-making discussed in earlier chapters – which included justifying and making excuses for personal behavior and trying to find meaning in highly stressful, even traumatic, personal events. Our contention is that such a motivated intellective functioning is prominent in the telling of myths and family stories. Certainly, in family stories, there may bc a tendency to distort memory in the service of the story-teller or loved ones. But it seems that there is an even greater drive toward a *flow with nature* associated with myths and family stories. (See Csikszentmihalyi (1975) for a related use of this term in connection with people's quest to conquer boredom and anxiety in their lives; his work will be discussed further in chapter 8.) It is a drive that probably has more resonance with the voices our ancestors may have heard thousands of years ago than it does with the well-springs of our psychologically-oriented modern society and its incessant focus on analyzing the reasons for behavior. Jaynes (1976), near the conclusion of his book, takes a more limiting position regarding any present semblance of ancient right-brain functioning:

> As individuals we are at the mercies of our collective imperatives (including the doctrine in many of the world's religions of the fall from divine favor). We see over our everyday attentions, our gardens and politics, and children, into the forms of our culture darkly. And our culture is our history. In our attempts to communicate or to persuade or simply interest others, we are using and moving about through cultural models among whose differences we may select, but from whose totality we cannot escape. And it is in this sense of the

forms of appeal, of begetting hope or interest or appreciation or praise for ourselves or for our ideas, that our communications are shaped into these historical patterns, these grooves of persuasion which are even in the act of communication an inherent part of what is communicated. And this essay is no exception. (Jaynes, 1976, p. 445)

In the end, the essence of this evolutionary perspective on account-making seems to be a conception of the possible role of accounts in helping solve three main metaproblems that confront humans, namely: *the search for meaning, the maintenance of morale, and the recognition of and negotiation with death.*

MEANING AND MORALITY

We began this chapter by suggesting that we would take the reader on a speculative odyssey about the evolutionary significance of account-making. We shall end the chapter in the same vein. Jaynes' thesis again is as a major part of our stimulus. We would argue that this new "I," to use Jaynes' and Mead's connotations, is here to stay as part of the evolution of humans. As such, the narratization activity of the "I" has become an essential part of civilization because of the increasing interdependence of human beings on this planet. Well over 3,000 years ago, the moral order of conduct may not have been so important to early humans who were relatively isolated from one another. That state of affairs changed as humans began to occupy overlapping territories, with conflict over resources (whether space, food, partners, or whatever) a natural result of this overlap. Today and well into the future, the world situation is one of intense and expanding interdependence among humans. We suggest that account-making is (sometimes in the form of myths and family stories) *one of the most essential elements* in the maintenance of a moral order in this situation. Human conflict and the resolution of conflict require that people justify theirs or others' actions, or fail to justify them, and more generally develop accounts for why certain actions are taken and how to deal with them. As the world situation becomes one of more interlocking interests, account-making in turn should become more refined and variegated among individuals, groups, and nations. In this light, account-making is a crucial hallmark of civilized life.

Thus, a summary point is that not only is the account helpful in enhancing meaning, morale, and direction for individuals as they face the stresses of life including the inevitability of their own and their loved ones' deaths, but also it becomes a key part of the glue that makes culture and civilization possible at the group level. In the media, international relations, everyday conversations and private thinking, we increasingly are "a psychological account-making, account-bearing, and -reporting species." Hence, choosing to return to greater right-brain functioning and the related reduction of narratization may not be that adaptive nor even possible if human interaction continues in the direction of becoming more and more characterized by the concept of "world village." Accordingly, given our logic about the contribution of accounts and account-making to civilization, we would argue that in the future social scientists should value and study more fully these concepts and phenomena as part of their central foci for understanding human social behavior.

SUMMARY

This chapter has involved a speculative analysis of evolutionary aspects of account-making. Jaynes' (1976) acclaimed thesis about the origin of consciousness was examined. It was suggested that with the advent of consciousness, the need to develop accounts became a part of the human condition. This 'narratization' process, as Jaynes calls it, serves the interest of feelings of personal control, responsibility, and freedom in a modern world that inherently offers no promises for such comforts. We also discussed McClelland's (1986) conception of two different types of love, one that is right-hemispheric dominant and one that is left-hemispheric dominant, and examples of the literatures of cognitive social psychology that, like work on account-making, also involve an emphasis on left-brain functioning. Finally, relationships among myths, family stories, and accounts were examined. In the next chapter, we shall elaborate on the *forms* that account-making may take, and the implications of such culture-wide manifestation for a broader multidisciplinary study of accounts.

7   Accounts in Literary Form

In our first several chapters we introduced the concept of accounts, loosely defining that concept and supporting our characterization with material from a variety of literatures, both popular and scholarly. We then (in chapter 3) presented our contribution to theoretical development in understanding and predicting account-making and its content. There followed three chapters exploring the account-making concept in applied contexts: in person perception, grief work, and a broader evolutionary perspective on narratization and the (sometimes) conscious quest for meaning. We turn in this chapter, just prior to concluding this monograph, to broadening our view of accounts beyond the disciplinary bounds of social science (within which, it is true, we have hardly felt it necessary to constrain ourselves, thus far anyway). It is our hope that some of these ideas will be not only provocative but intriguing, and will prove so inviting and *accessible* to the scholar-reader that others will feel similarly inspired to see accounts in many venues and endeavors.

For the study of accounts is a very projective exercise: we begin to see, and seek to confirm, accounts and account-like forms and functions in every context and situation. We pick up a newspaper and read a journalist's *account* of a tragedy, punctuated with the *accounts* of individual survivors, who themselves illustrate their tales with the *accounts* fellow travelers or less fortunate mates have confided in them. Every poem tells a story; in every piece of fiction or non-fiction we hear the voice of the writer or singer, expressing his or her own secret history, sharing it so that, while subtle, it will no longer be so secret.

In this chapter we argue that commonalities exist among individuals' accounts in part because they participate in a much larger, culture-wide and cross-cultural tradition of storytelling. Each person's account is in a way a microcosm of the larger human story; cultural myths ring true because they consist of a collectivity of personal legends. Thus many accounts break through, or beyond, individual story-forming and story-telling efforts, and show up in the various expressive forms within and across cultures. This is what we mean by accounts "in literary form": accounts expressed – and received – not as individual stories shared with intimates, but in more public (i.e. accessible to strangers) shapes and genres. Thus accounts can and will be found as or within forms of literature (short stories, novels, plays, poetry), journalism (histories, biography, and autobiography), and popular culture (songs, humor, essays, films, and television). In this chapter we explore the function of literary accounts, some of the themes common in accounts in literary form, and some conclusions about the pervasiveness of an account-making "drive." We begin our exploration with three general arguments: accounts are compelling; their telling is sparked by change or crisis; the precise form they take is influenced by numerous personal and situational factors.

CHARACTERISTICS OF LITERARY ACCOUNTS

Accounts are Compelling

At the beginning of *Fireflies*, David Morrell (1988) asserts that he will tell his story, of the death of his young son, with "terrible compulsion, . . . driven to describe that ordeal" (Morrell, 1988, p. 4). Morrell recalls in his own behavior the spectre of Coleridge's Ancient Mariner, cursed to wander and assail strangers with his frenzied, woeful rhyme. Many accounts seem to take literary form as the result of such a force within the poet or artist who then applies the tools of the trade to refine somewhat the final form. Thus, for example, journalist Inette Miller (1987) kept a diary of her mid-life affair – an experience that jarred and shattered her life and the lives of her loved ones – but then transformed that diary into a book, published for others' eyes. Toward the end she acknowledges the effect of this change in form:

This diary is going to end here. It's not going to end as it began – with a concrete event, titillation – the big bang . . . This diary ends today because I've sold it for publication as a book–and that effectively ends it. There are eyes reading over my shoulder now and I become self-conscious. There is an audience, and my writing reacts to that – the spontaneity and honesty of the journal are gone. (Miller, 1987, p. 236)

Miller alludes interestingly to the *loss* of honesty incurred by making her account public – literally, by *publication*. Yet the beginning of her diary/book is disarmingly fresh and ingenuous, clearly not the exercise of a professional journalist vying for a private readership. Even as she embarked on the shaky course of her attraction to and affair with a married man, Miller turned to wordcraft to spill, and spell, her experiences out.

Different expertise translates accounts into different media. Recently the, film-maker Ingmar Bergman commented on the fact that another director has committed himself to film Bergman's story of his own parents' marriage. In an interview, Bergman explained that he felt a "great need to tell the story" of his parents' relationship, observing that they seemed "predestined for catastrophe" because of pressures and demands in their lives (Associated Press, 1989).

Journalists keep journals, film-makers create screenplays. It has been observed by many a writing instructor that first-time writers always begin with autobiography – perhaps never to abandon or move beyond that subject matter. It may be that accounts in literary form reflect a naivete or narcissism. But professional journalists and filmmakers hardly typify such egocentrism. They could find and have found many non-self subjects for their work. Why incorporate a personal account into one's script or essay series if that story were not in itself compelling at some level?

Further, not all accounts are explicitly self-serving, even if they are close to home in subject matter, dealing with one's most familiar or familial relations and experiences. A recent news feature reported that a nine-year-old boy was found by his mother to be writing not a homework assignment, but a personal recollection of a young playmate who had died of cancer when both boys were only six:

I had a friend named Marcel. Every time he came over to my house to play we always did fun things together. We both grew up together. We went to preschool together and we went to kindergarten together. The best time we ever had was when I slept over at his house for the first time . . . And I remember all the good times we had and I feel like Marcel is there with me. And if I had one wish, just one wish, it would be to bring Marcel back to life. (Greene, 1989)

The young boy was not trained in journalism or creative writing. But he was a schoolboy, with a student's habits, and these were the tools he used to give form to his account of friendship and loss.

The compellingness of accounts may take the form of a seeming "autobiographical urge," a writer's desire to self-disclose or self-refer in the course of making other or more general points. This urge may be ill-formed or vague, inappropriate or discomfortingly intimate. But when we read it in a short story, or recognize it in a song, it can be arrestingly real and riveting. In short, one may feel as compelled to pay attention to it as the account-maker felt to give it form and voice in the first place.

Literary Accounts are Precipitated

We argued in chapter 3 that, while the vast motives, speculations, semi-articulated emotions and attributions that make up one's account may accumulate over years of experience, they are not necessarily "packaged" – much less so presented – until and unless triggered by relevant stressor events. Thus a woman, on being rejected by a lover, confides to a friend or therapist *for the first time* the fact that she had hopes for the relationship, unrealistic fantasies for its meaning in her life, and suspicions and dreads of its futility. The realization and expression of these thoughts and feelings is new, but presumably they have underlain much of her actions and words up to this point.

To extend that process to literary accounts, we might suggest that a writer, for example, has collected many threads of an account-like story in her life, but pulls them together and presents them coherently only when she has become inspired by a real-life prompt to write it down, or a plot- or character-development *within* her writing that provides inspiration as well as a vehicle for this particular package. The "iceberg" of the account – the massive, submerged bulk of ideas and motives – accrues and weighs, but does not surface, not until it is "time." When it *is* time, the account rendition may not be deliberately concocted, but rather well up from the author's experience. Consider, for example, the richness of sentiment and spontaneity captured in Baudelaire's poem, "Le Flacon," a rumination on the potency of the past:

> Il est de forts parfums pour qui toute matière
> Est poreuse. On dirait qu'ils penètrent la verre.
> En ouvrant un coffret venu de l'Orient
> Dont la serrure grince et rechigne en criant.

Ou dans une maison deserte quelque armoire
Pleine de l'acre odeur des temps, poudreuse et noire,
Parfois on trouve un vieux flacon qui se souvient,
D'ou jaillit toute vive une ame qui revient.

There are strong perfumes for which all matter
Is porous. You might say they penetrate the glass.
Opening a coffer from the Orient
Whose lock grates and cries sulkily

Or in a deserted house an armoire
Filled with the acrid odor of time, dusty and black,
Sometimes one finds an old perfume bottle that remembers,
From which springs forth in all its freshness a soul
  returning.[1]

This image of the past returning to pervade present experience is a frequent and powerful one in literary accounts. In a very different genre and use, writers of short stories reveal their characters' (or their own) introspection about the power of the past returning. For example, at the end of Ann Beattie's short story, "The Big Outside World": Renee listens as her husband Tadd good-naturedly recalls an episode from his youth, when he had sought privacy so he and his girlfriend could be alone. Renee quizzes him about what else happened between them, and Tadd expresses surprise that she might be jealous of "something I did when I was a teenager." Renee muses privately that such jealousy is entirely reasonable because "people and things never really get left behind" and one would forever be surprised into remembering them (Beattie, 1986). Here Beattie comments poignantly on the sudden resurgence of memory, the insistence of the past on intruding or abiding in one's present. And if it is one's partner's past, it may be unknown and yet irrepressibly *there*, present and persuasive in the relationship.

Although the expression of a particular memory or perception within a literary account may be prompted by an evocative experience, such as a stressor or revelation, the talent of the artist or writer can certainly be brought to bear on the final form given to that expression. Thus although the original story might have been raw, ill-shaped, ineffable, its final form is relatively polished, neat, even standardized, so that it may seem completely fabricated, deliberately composed, rather than prompted or elicited. In the short poem, "Ein Leben" (A Life), the poet Dan Pagis (1989) reconstructs his interpretation of what is happening in a photograph taken of his mother when he was a small boy. She died within the month, and in the poem Pagis interprets the qualities of the photograph–her appearance, her mood, the lights and shadows–as portending the fragility of her life and the imminence of her departure. The poet describes a reconstruction of his own past, a moment of cherishment occasioned by reflecting on an old photograph. Accounts can be stirred up by reminders, disturbances of the smooth surface of present routine and relationships. Part of the "work" of the account is to reinterpret the stirred-up fragments of recollection in light of latter-day maturity, understanding, or forgiveness.

Influences on the Form of Literary Accounts

The form taken by accounts (as if they take them on themselves) is governed by myriad factors and influences. One of these is the cultural context in which the writer or speaker is working. For example, although Woody Allen has written many short stories, he is best known for his work in films, most of which deal with the tragi-comedy of personal relationships. In another time or place, with facility in another technology, Allen's themes might be translated not into film but into novels, sculpture, poetry, or journalism. Subcultural expectations might further influence the account-maker's form of expression: letter-writing and diaries might be appropriate for a particular age or age group, while another might encourage song-writing or rap routines instead. Certainly the personal articulateness of the account-maker will affect the literary form chosen and the refinement it attains. Recall from chapter 5 the example of the 68−year-old teacher who, fifteen years after her mother's death, felt moved on thinking about her to write a poem to her. Presumably she had not previously considered herself a poet, but for precious sentiments and in respect for the fragility of her own feelings, she felt it important to structure her thoughts in that form. Others might choose a less verbal memorial, like a photograph album or a sentimental quote embroidered in needlepoint. Finally, the very form of a literary account may simply be a matter of the media of facility: what material is handy with which to construct my story? What substances and shapes seem closest to the material of memory?

An important consideration in the composition of a literary account seems to be that of the *audience*, their expectations and motives. Is the account-maker talking to a stranger he or she hopes to impress or please? Are we chatting with acquaintances at the funeral of a mutual friend? Our words have not only a source but a goal: once sprung from our own thoughts and feelings, how do they strike the receiving audience? Here lies the critical difference between, say, keeping a diary in shorthand – for one's own eyes and reference alone – and composing an autobiography (or researching an "unauthorized biography" of an admired figure) ultimately for the consumption and curiosity of others. Inette Miller captures this audience awareness early in her own meta-accounting: "Today I feel a real need to write. I seem to be able to think things out on paper, and that helps. I wonder who my audience for this journal of thoughts will be." She goes on to admit an expectation that she is writing down her thoughts and experiences for her husband to read one day, an acknowledgement that sharing with him has become a strong habit and something she hopes to do again.

Miller acknowledges what most biographers and autobiographers either assume or leave unsaid: the fact that readers of the work are self-selected and already moved to "read on" by their own personal curiosities and fascination with the subject. Reading, like writing, is filtered through layers of interpretation and prejudice. We have earlier (chapter 1) quoted William Runyan (1982) as noting that there is no such thing as a "definitive" biography. The very act of writing/reading becomes the record of the moment; "saying is believing." The account's rendition becomes the "way it happened." Accounts may take the form of an entire literary work, as in biography or autobiography. In recent years it seems more and more celebrated persons are composing their own "memoirs" rather early in their lives and careers, as if to put the stamp of ownership on events as they would have them understood. Different versions of a life may be produced and promoted at the same time, as happened after the death of the actor Rock Hudson from AIDS, and after writer Kitty Kelley published her "unauthorized" (and unflattering) biography of Frank Sinatra, closely followed by Nancy Sinatra's own, more sympathetic, *My Father: Frank Sinatra*. The novel, historically a recent literary form, may be the best known form suitable to account-making. Within the world created by the writer of the novel, the process of account-making itself can be scrutinized and frankly acknowledged, as in this excerpt from Kurt Vonnegut's novel, *Mother Night*:

> I was a fairly successful playwright, writing in the language in which I write best, German . . .
> I was sitting alone on a park bench in the sunshine that day, thinking of a fourth play that was beginning to write itself in my mind. It gave itself a title, which was "*Das Reich der Zwei*," – "Nation of Two." It was going to be about

the love my wife and I had for each other. It was going to show how a pair of lovers in a world gone mad could survive by being loyal only to a nation composed of themselves – a nation of two (Vonnegut, 1966, p. 37).

Here Vonnegut seems to be acknowledging the "autobiographical urge" in his own work. That urge can take the forms of poems, plays, and screenplays. We might even consider the "urge" as it shows up in less artistic compositions, such as letters to advice and lonely-hearts columnists. For example, two newspaper columnists soliciting readers' stories under the byline "Tales from the Front" received the following:

We're both in our middle forties, married for 25 years, not to each other. We fell in love 25 years ago. But after a few months, Walt was notified by a girl that he had gotten her pregnant. Being the wonderful person that he is, he married her. We continued seeing each other, even though I wanted to die. After a while, I knew we had no future, only more hurt, so I walked away. Within a year I married a man, not knowing he was an alcoholic with an awful temper. I went to Al-Anon to learn to live with him. He's like a bomb, always ready to go off. I always wondered what happened to Walt. When I was in the malls, I'd look for him. One day he walked up to me, just like I'd hoped and prayed. We are in love, but love hurts so bad. I don't know what will happen. His life hasn't been as awful as mine, but he says he never stopped loving me . . . (in Kavesh and Lavin, 1989, p. 2–2).

Similar accounts can be found in the columns of newspapers and magazines that occasionally invite readers to submit their own stories for "special issues" dedicated to Valentine's Day or holiday seasons. Whatever images of pathos and self-destruction might be conjured by stories like the one above, it does seem that we return to a point we have tried to make about accounts: accounts seem to be "right there," below but near the surface of the account-maker's consciousness, and in some state of readiness to be related, shared, or presented. Kavesh and Lavin's example may lack art, but it is too jumbled and self-deprecating to be contrived or disingenuous. Were this "author's" motives for seeing her words in print so very different from those of a more professional writer?

FUNCTIONS OF LITERARY ACCOUNTS

The accounts embedded in literary forms may be elaborately and deliberately so placed, but for the most part are probably part of a writer's less conscious armamentarium. They appear in fragments, in phrases or paragraphs rather than entire subplots, the essences of longer stories which we refer to in chapter 8 as "gists." Accounts may serve as a vehicle or illustration for the writer or composer, who in turn provides them as a service or pedagogic device for his or her readers. Such literary accounts serve many, many functions, only three of which we shall consider and illustrate here: justification, characterization, and rapport.

Rationalization and Justification

An account is often woven into a story to ground someone's (the writer's or a character's) motives, building up to a pinch-point or climax. For example, in Laurie Colwin's novel *Family Happiness*, Polly talks with her secret lover, Lincoln, about her feelings regarding her family, including her guilt over having betrayed her husband Henry by having this affair with Lincoln in the first place. In a brief exchange, Lincoln summarizes for Polly his impressions of her family based on his conviction that, when she met him, she was obviously neglected and love-starved. Far from being the innocent victims of Polly's deception, her family are, for Lincoln, the culprits who drove her into the arms of another. Lincoln goes on to give his view, his account, of Polly's family life, a version that not only exonerates her for having sought authentic happiness outside her marriage, but questions her intelligence in having waited so long to do so. The character of Lincoln is only now speaking his mind, but has made his observations and drawn his conclusions, his own rationalizations about the wisdom of the affair from Polly's perspective, *all along*. His tacit understandings are only packaged into this angry diatribe when he has had enough of Polly's self-berating for violating the trust of her "loving family."

Justification need not be the all-consuming focus of a literary form; a justificatory account can appear in abbreviated form, almost like a cliché, a suggestion, a "gist," in quickly establishing for a reader the sense of characters' backgrounds, action, and milieu. In his most recent espionage novel, John Le Carré summarizes one such moment of truth, in describing the first meeting between the protagonist, Barley, a cynical British publisher working in an intelligence operation, and Katya, his only contact with a dissident writer. The reader knows that Barley and Katya are destined to become lovers, but "When they met they surprised each other. After all, they were still strangers, closer to the forces that had brought them here than to one another" (1989, p. 133). In this brief passage – merely a gist, an intimation of an account – Le Carré acknowledges the invisible forces and factors working to entwine two lives, and the suspension of those dynamics in time yet to come.

More commonly, authors may provide a capsule summary of *past* events, fictional or real, to see (or impose) an inevitable order in them that was not possible earlier or in close observation. For example, Miller introduces the diary/novelization of her own mid-life affair by tersely ticking-off the events preceding her diary's account: When her infant son became a toddler she began to write again; she worked for months on a project and sent it to a publisher. And, as a natural extension of this growth process, she began her affair. This almost clinical listing, a brief background to her own case history, is the extent of Miller's apologia for her subsequently diarized behavior. The justification is implicit in her listing of the affair as one of a series of "projects" that have apparently served to answer her own generativity crisis.

Characterization

Accounts can also be used to explain (as opposed to excuse) characters' behavior and experiences; to enrich the history of a scene or plot development; to bring the reader "up to date" on the dramatic or comic action. In a short story entitled "Slippage" John Updike uses an abbreviated account to explain the character and current crises of Morison, a history professor past his own possibilities. Morison's wife was a former student of his; he was a history professor; on this last day of term his lecture is rewarded with customary student applause; and he reflects on his own career and its failure to earn a note in history. Update achieves volumes of characterization and caricature in only a few lines of Morison's reflection and intropection, because of the power and richness of the life-story. In this particular case, Updike's characterization of Morison is somewhat cerebral, with the emphasis on his work and career. But an essential component of many accounts is *emotion*, whether painted with restraint or with broad, colorful strokes, to reveal the depth of feeling within the character or the author. In the last stanza of 'Broken Vows,' by the nineteenth-century Irish poet, Lady Augusta Gregory, a young woman expresses both pain and numbness at being abandoned by her lover:

You have taken the East from me, you have taken the West
  from me.

You have taken what is before me and what is behind me.
You have taken the moon, you have taken the sun from me,
And my fear is great you have taken God from me.

Accounts in literary form may argue different "versions" of real-life events. In the first stanza of "Fare Thee Well!" Lord Byron implies that he has been wronged by Fate and arbitrarily rejected and cast off by his judgemental wife:

Fare thee well! and if for ever,
Still for ever, fare thee well:
Even though unforgiving, never
   'Gainst thee shall my heart rebel.[2]

Not to be outdone, Lady Byron composed her own 'Reply,' and concluded with this last correction of the records:

But farewell! I'll not upbraid thee
   Never, never wish thee ill;
Wretched tho' thy crimes have made me,
   If thou canst – be happy still.[3]

Literary Tone: Establishing Rapport

Professional writers speak *to* an audience. One function of the account in literary form is to assist in establishing rapport with the reader or listener, to respond to the audience's real (or imagined) needs for empathy, reflection, or comradeship with the account-maker. Research on the persuasive power of the vivid anecdote tells us that such emotion-laden stories can be more moving than rational argument. A familiar account can powerfully involve an audience member more effectively than a list of reasons explaining why the writer might "deserve" a reader's attention. In a poem that was clearly designed to be read aloud, Judith Steinbergh begins with the title, 'There Are No Rules':

and my ex-husband on his fortieth birthday shows up to
pick up his sister who is visiting me and brings his
   girlfriend
who is still in college leaving her on my front porch
   to chat
about her major while he runs upstairs to shower and my
lover comes to observe my daughter's classroom with his ex-
wife who is not even his ex-wife yet while I am there
   visiting

and we are cordial, we are more than cordial, we are intimate
  in this irony. . . . (1988, p. 18).

This example may express the importance of literary form, or of the specific form chosen, in relating the account. As a poem, 'There Are No Rules' can tell the speaker's relationship story (or stories!) in a run-on fashion, conversationally, intimately with her audience. Surely the same themes in short story or novel would fall more heavily, be weighed down with the structure of establishing character, plot, and crisis in addition to tone.

Accounts may also help to establish a more intimate tone between author and reader because the *fact* of the account presents the author as deserving of the reader's attention and appreciation. In chapter 4, it has been suggested that some individuals may be more sensitive to the fact that someone is relating his or her account – self-disclosing, insightful, vulnerable – than to whatever unpleasant admissions may be found within the account itself. It is as if the writer were saying, "I know I'm not a sympathetic character and I've done wrong, but here I am telling you my story in my own words. Doesn't that count for something?"

THEMES OF LITERARY ACCOUNTS

Accounts in literary form can be found to convey a wide variety of identifiable themes. A content analysis of accounts in literary form can yield much information about writers and readers, and assumptions about both writers and readers. We review here examples of several such themes: memorializing; self-presentation; making sense; entertainment; and making peace with oneself and others.

Memorializing

By far the most common, almost incessant, theme of accounts in literary form is that of commemorating the past. The theme of remembering in literary accounts emphasizes the importance (to the rememberer) of remembering *as an end in itself* rather than a mere means to other ends like rationalization, self-satisfaction, or self-presentation. Memorializing can be focused on an anniversary, as it is in the last pages of Miller's affair diary, in which she counts the passage of time (one year) since the beginning of her world-changing affair with David Muller–and agonizes about the ambivalence she feels about wanting to share the remembrance with him, but not wanting to be the one who makes the call–or the appeal.

A more familiar form for such commemoration is the sort of collective remembering presented in memoirs that take in the multiplicity of characters and places a writer considers. Susan Allen Toth has written two such works, *Blooming* (1981), about her formative years in Iowa, and *Ivy Days* (1984), about going to college in the East. Although she changed the names, the characters were recognizable – perhaps too recognizable, since even persons she did *not* remember later wrote to her, insisting that they had "found themselves" in her books. It is apparently important not only to remember the past, but also to *be* remembered. In *Ivy Days,* for example Toth commemorates a good friend, who had changed but not for the better, in the twelve years since graduation. The friend, Chris, had made a surprise visit to Toth, who was disturbed at how Chris had altered: she had gained weight, she drank too much, and despite her claims of a busy career and social life, she seemed bitter about having met her life-goals too early. Two years after this encounter, Toth read Chris's obituary in their alumnae magazine: Chris had died of a liver ailment at the age of 37.

Sometimes the commemoration expresses a sort of grief for oneself, for being left alone with memories no one else shares. In "The Passing of Thistle," the poet Peter Davison (1989) addresses just this loss and longing for remembrance in grieving after the death of a pet (in this case a beloved dog) whom the poem credits with sharing, if not recounting, the poet's memories. The poem was published in the September 1989 edition of *The Atlantic:* in the December issue were published several letters that praise Davison's poem and go on to explain in some detail their own memories of – and grief over – their own pets. Worth noting is the "begetting" effect of such a grief/account poem on others: readers are moved to write their own appreciations, for the benefit of still other readers (who may note this effect in writings about grief, literature, and account-making).

Self-presentation

None the less self-presentation is a popular and familiar theme in literary accounts. By revealing one's background (the author's or a character's), even in an abbreviated package, one says, "This is who I am" and "This is why you should care about me." Some such accounts will pursue ulterior motives of manipulating the readers' (or other characters') affections. Others will more simply self-reveal and leave it up to the audience to decide whether and how the revelation will take effect. In *Daybook: Journal of an Artist*, Anne Truitt (1982) conveys a powerful sense of what it means to be an artist, not by ceaselessly explaining herself to unknown readers, but by revealing her deepest discoveries and concerns in simple admissions. In one journal entry Truitt reflects on her sorrow earlier in the day upon her realization that a cherished series of paintings, recently sold, will remain after her in the world, while her own life and identity will end. Her joy in the endurance and value of her work is tempered by her confrontation with mortality and the drain of productivity. Truitt's brief diary entry powerfully expresses the paradox of what the neo-Freudian psychologist Erik Erikson (1963)) called the "generativity crisis," the struggle to leave something of worth and permanence behind one's own brief lifetime. The irony is that you can't "leave" something behind without "leaving" or departing yourself. However unrefined, this characterization of the writer – and the artists she represents – stays with the reader for the remainder of the journal.

The person-perception power of accounts is also illustrated in James Joyce's short story, 'The Dead,' the last piece in his classic collection of character studies, *Dubliners* (1916). In this story, a married couple, Gabriel and Gretta, attend a dinner party, where Gretta becomes distracted by a ballad sung by one of the guests. Alone later and preparing for bed, she tearfully tells Gabriel that the song reminded her of a boy she knew when she was young, a boy who had died for love of her, and whom she continued to mourn:

> She was fast asleep.
> Gabriel, leaning on his elbow, looked for a few moments unresentfully on her tangled hair and half-open mouth, listening to her deep-drawn breath. So she had had that romance in her life: a man had died for her sake. It hardly pained him now to think how poor a part he, her husband, had played in her life. He watched her while she slept as though he and she had never lived together as man and wife. His curious eyes rested long upon her face and on her hair: and, as he thought of what she must have been then, in that time of her first girlish beauty, a strange friendly pity entered his soul. (1916 pp. 221–2)

Gabriel looks at Gretta in an entirely new way in light of this account of hers, the sad story of her long-ago lost love. Gabriel enters a new present after hearing his wife's past. Accounts in literary form – and within the bounds of the literary work – reshape the world for those work – reshape the world for those persons or characters who receive them, by altering their perceptions of the account-giver.

Making Sense

Literary accounts, just like real-life accounts, are called into service to make sense out of one's experiences, to help establish the meaning in one's life. We have previously (chapter 2) quoted Shotter (1987) about the value of "retrospectively making sense" of one's own experiences. One form of such sense-making involves portraying a person's (or character's) experiences as being *inevitable*, as though the context were scripted, the actor had no choice, and what seemed spontaneous at the time has in fact turned out to be one more subplot within a powerful pattern. In her novel *Postcards from the Edge*, Carrie Fisher tells the story of a young actress, Suzanne Vale, who has been beleaguered by drug dependency and disappointing relationships. In an excerpt from her diary in the detoxification unit, Suzanne observes:

> I envy people who have the capacity to sit with another human being and find them endlessly interesting. I would rather watch TV. Of course, this eventually becomes known to the other person. I once told Jonathan that I would pay more attention to him if he got better programming. It always seems that in the beginning with someone, nothing they do could ever be wrong, except that they don't see you enough. And eventually it gets to the point where you just want to say, "Get off my leg, okay?" (Fisher, 1987, p. 20).

Suzanne is describing *all* relationships, not just her own. For Suzanne, individual relationships participate in a larger dance of relationships, such that each new partnership, begun uniquely, is caught up in the cadence of the others, and destined to go through the same movements and stages. In characterizing humans as narrative-knowers and storytellers (see Read, 1987), we see that stories themselves – whether sketchy scripts or elaborate stage productions – offer possibilities for purpose in life.

Entertainment

An important theme in literary accounts is entertainment, by the account-maker, for his or her audience – or for him- or herself. Given the function of accounts in establishing rapport with one's readers or listeners, entertainment may be the most prevalent theme in published accounts. In Nora Ephron's 1983 novel *Heartburn*, based closely and poignantly on the breakdown of her own marriage to the news reporter Carl Bernstein, Ephron's protagonist/alter-ego Rachel argues with her therapist, Vera, about making a joke out of the painful events in her life:

> Vera said: "Why do you feel you have to turn everything into a story?"
> So I told her why:
> Because if I tell the story, I control the version.
> Because if I tell the story, I can make you laugh and I would rather have you laugh at me than feel sorry for me.
> Because if I tell the story, it doesn't hurt as much.
> Because if I tell the story, I can get on with it. (Ephron, 1983, pp. 176–7).

One of the author's colleague's comments that he has come to think of his past relationships as having been this or that partner's "regime," implying the dictatorial and arbitrary rules different women have imposed on his life and household. This is not a full-fledged account, but it does capture the essence of relationship stories, perhaps only in conveying the "gist" of this man's relationship history, as he relates it for the enjoyment and instruction of his listeners. This is probably an obvious function of account-making in all our lives: what is more surely entertaining to our friends than our own self-deprecating recollections of the gaffes we have committed in the name of love?

In her research on family stories, Elizabeth Stone (1988) extends the entertainment theme by describing how once-sketchy anecdotes about ancestors or offspring will be embellished, added to a family's repertoire, and trotted out to entertain the guests at family get-togethers. In the telling and retelling, with exaggerations and nuances to impress or amuse the audience, these new versions take on a life of their own, and resist any later paring down or streamlining to their original, less entertaining form.

Making Peace

Tied in with a need for justification is often a quest for forgiveness and understanding. The account-maker/storyteller lays out a chronicle of his or her experiences, showing how events "had" to transpire, perhaps asking forgiveness. Some "inside stories" have more of a sense of confession than of confiding. In her book *It's*

Always Something, the late comedienne Gilda Radner describes her experiences battling with the cancer that ultimately took her life shortly after her book was published. She recalls the irony of once having developed comedy routines that ridiculed cancer and death, only now to be facing those fears herself, without the insulation of humor: with wry candor she concludes "it came back to haunt me" (Radner, 1989, p. 100)

Thompson and Janigian (1988) observe that life schemata provide a framework for understanding people's search for meaning, that a life schema tells the story with oneself as protagonist. Similarly, in such examples as Gilda Radner's, the quest for exoneration or understanding articulates itself as a plea to the reader to keep a sense of perspective, to refrain from judging the subject any more harshly than she judges herself.

STORIES WITHIN STORIES: THE ACCOUNT-MAKING DRIVE

If, as we have argued, accounts are "compelling," then for many reasons, some of which we have explored here, we are *driven* to tell our stories. But is it always *our* stories we are moved to tell? Accounts cast into literary form seem other than real, less than frank. Are literary accounts merely a safe surrogate for our own?

We might speculate at this point on just which stories are "our" stories. Clearly the stories of our own lives are "our" stories. But we are generous, expansive: we claim others' stories as our own. In Walt Whitman's words: "I am large; I contain multitudes" (1982, p 246). The lives of those we love become "our" stories as well. How far does it go? It may be that lives within our culture are "ours" to recount in broader terms, in legend and myth, perhaps, rather than in chronicle or journal. In the process of retelling a simple anecdote we perceive a truth, a common bond with others, and in adding our story to the cultural repertoire, we also earn the right to borrow from that larger store of stories in weaving our own tales.

If accounts are compelling, then accounts, even in literary form, are not so much crafted as revealed. They bubble to the surface, seeking their own level, in spite of the author's efforts at disguise or containment. Maybe "all first works are autobiographical" not because all first-time writers are narcissistic but because all subsequent stories must follow from that first account, which has to be let go to release the others. Stories emerge into a final form because that is their *natural*, inevitable form. Michelangelo reputedly asserted that, when sculpting a form from marble, he did not so much impose a shape *onto* an unformed block as seek to discover the figure *within* the block, to see what it was meant to be, what shape it was meant to assume, and then chip away its cover to reveal it.

If accounts are compelling, and if "our" stories seek expression through us – in fiction if we are crafters of fiction, in diary entries if we are scribes – then *when* are these stories likely to emerge? In our review of family stories (chapter 6) we suggested that such stories function as a sort of familial glue, timely lessons in family integrity, useful to recite in times of stress and despair. In chapter 3 we developed our premise that account-making is most intense in "working through" and achieving "closure" in response to a stressor event. To extend this model from the individual to the cultural level, it seems plausible that a culture would use its storytelling forms most particularly in times of cultural stress and transition, much as an individual account-maker does in personal moments of questioning and crisis.

If accounts in literary form develop in response to cultural crisis, this will lead to developments in *many* genres, not only those forms recognized as literary (although literature is certainly the easiest genre to focus on here as reference and illustration). Cultural accounts will emerge in music, visual and theater arts, even informal scripts for personal interaction. In this chapter and earlier in this book, especially in chapter 2, we have reviewed a substantial amount of popular literature. Do people learn more readily from such stories? There is little doubt that stories themselves are unusually popular and fashionable now. Short stories in particular seem to be enjoying a renaissance. In the United States reader's theater, with professional actors reciting short stories, has become as popular as traditional plays, and radio programming, traditionally devoted to news and popular music, is now beginning to compete with television by offering stories, essays, and monologues without visual restrictions. Books on audiotape, once a rarity or available only for the blind, now command their own shelf space in bookshops. Whatever the reasons, and there are certainly many – such as the impatience of American 'Baby Boomers' to pore over long novels, the convenience of tuning into short stories on one's personal stereo rather than make eye contact with fellow travelers on public transport – stories are an enormously popular literary form. We have earlier quoted Robert Coles as advocating a "respect for narrative as everyone's rock-bottom capacity, but also as the universal gift, to be shared with others" (Coles, 1989, p. 30). Herein may lie much of the appeal of the literary account.

There has also been a resurgence of interest in the works of such scholars as Joseph Campbell (e.g. 1972, 1988), who used examples of myths to support his argument that myth pervades culture, crosses cultures, and traverses time and space to emerge, in form after form and through many retellings, to reveal the familiar and human. Our different cultural stories canonize the same fears, the same lessons, the same fantasies across human communities and ideologies. Has this always been the case? Why are short stories so fashionable *now*? Why only *now* is the work of the late American mythologist Joseph Campbell going into new editions and, on television in the United States, videotaped broadcasts, if his words have addressed a more timeless truth? It may be that we only tell or recognize the stories (individual or cultural) that ring true *for our time*. For example, a review of the recent films of Woody Allen, Oliver Stone, and Neil Simon comments on the autobiographical urge in each artist's material. Simon's *Brighton Beach Memoirs* recounted his own youth; his *Biloxi Blues* satirized his own memories of basic military training in a boot camp. Woody Allen's films – especially those about personal relationships – are always attributed to realities in his own experience or personality, despite his repeated protests that they are more fictional than autobiographical. Oliver Stone directed and wrote the screenplay for *Platoon*, one of the first and few post-Vietnam films to portray the horror and ambiguities of the war, based largely on his own experiences there. A reviewer comparing the films of Stone, Allen, and Simon, has suggested that the "nakedly confessional" *Platoon* earned its enormous following because the director's compulsion to tell his story resonates with a culture-wide need to do the same (*USA Today*, 1987). Thus, while stories and accounts with various themes and conclusions may be related and recorded *all* the time, perhaps it is only when we as a culture are *primed* to see or hear a particular story that we receive it with appreciation and praise.

Finally, the goals and functions of storytelling and literature have obviously changed over the millennia. Debates continue, for example, about whether prehistoric cave paintings of bison and deer originally functioned as records of successful hunts, or as icons for pre-hunt inspiration, or merely as targets for spear-throwing practice. For that matter, academic courses titled 'The Bible as History' or 'The Bible as Literature' suggest that there is not universal consensus on whether the "function" of scripture is or was chronology or allegory. For accounts in literary form, the function matters. The literary account is shaped by its goal, its intended lesson. The villains who broke our hearts are painted larger than life; the saviors who taught us to love again are superhumanly virtuous and attractive. Accounts of love, like love itself, blend the real with the ideal. John Lukacs observes that modern storytelling respects the value of accuracy and veridicality far more than was ever previously the case:

> Our consciousness of history has grown to the extent where the historical form of thought envelops not only the legendary past but portions close to the present, because they are *real*—while our more remote ancestors cultivated a vision of the past that was *ideal* (Lukacs, 1970, p. 214).

CONCLUSION: ACCOUNT-MAKING AND ACCOUNT-TAKING

Account-making appears to take both expressive *and receptive* forms: we actively account-make by seeking and resonating with the "right" stories, even if authored by others, as well as by relating our own. We learn from literature, we draw conclusions and apply lessons not only to our stories but to our lives as well. We are consumers as well as constructors of accounts. We tell our own stories; that is the clearest form of account-making, but it is only *one* form. We also read the stories (watch the films) others have fabricated for our viewing. Both the telling and the reading (viewing, reciting, etc.) of these literary forms of accounts manifest the inner responsiveness we experience to our personal legends, within our larger cultural family of myths. We are satisfied, or vindicated, or relieved, when we can tell our stories and be heard and accepted. But it appears we are no less gratified to "find" a story – or a fragment or gist of one – which seems in part to be "ours" as well, though we have not been the first to tell it.

Accounts in literary form are compelling, are composed in response to a moment of crisis or need, and take (or are given) form according to the context within which they emerge. We have reviewed the justifying, characterizing, and tone-setting functions of literary accounts. And we have considered examples of a number of themes in literary accounts. In the concluding chapter, we shall end our exploration of accounts with an examination of our stress-response model of account-making, and a consideration of the role of the account in the broader contexts of self-identity and social influence.

SUMMARY

The study of accounts is a projective experience: accounts and account-making can be identified in literary forms as well as in personal introspection or social exchange. Personal accounts will be influenced by prevailing cultural myths and popular stories. Literary accounts are compelling, in that authors will find stories and anecdotes a natural and necessary way to communicate, just as readers will find such material personally engaging and relevant. Literary accounts may be precipitated by a stressful experience or an emotional allusion. They are influenced by such factors as what modes of expression are technologically possible or culturally encouraged. Literary accounts will also be influenced by the anticipated nature of the readership and the literary form in which they appear. Accounts in literary form may serve a variety of functions: justification of a course of action; fuller characterization of individuals described; and the establishment of greater rapport with the reader. Finally, literary accounts can be found to concentrate on several common themes: memorializing; self-presentation; making sense; entertainment; and making peace with oneself and others. Account-making is influenced and characterized by larger cultural mythology, fantasies, and life lessons. Account-making thus appears to take on both expressive and receptive forms, and we respond to others' accounts in the same way that we feel moved to compose and share our own.

8 Finale: Evaluating Our Account of Account-making

Gilda Radner described in *New Woman Magazine* (July 1989), the importance to her of her book *It's Always Something* (1989), published just prior to her death from cancer:

> I wanted to share the feelings I was going through, the fear at the beginning, the crying, all of it. When I got sick I looked around for things to validate my experience and I couldn't find them. I read Jill Ireland's story about her cancer, and when my hair fell out from chemotherapy, I wanted desperately to see a picture of Jill without any hair – to know I wasn't alone. But she didn't put one in her book. So in my book, I put in all the things I'd wanted to know about the disease and its treatment – including a picture of bald Gilda . . . I got a great sense of control from doing the project, from collecting my thoughts. Anything you can do to get back in charge of your life aids in recovery. (1989, p. 122)

In this book, we have suggested that the account-making activity is a crucial human enterprise. It often represents, as it did for Gilda Radner, the human's finest hour – the presentation of some aspect of one's own life and experiences that may help both self and others cope with problems of towering magnitude. We have reviewed past conceptual and empirical analyses of the concepts of accounts and account-making in social psychology. We have provided extentions of this work with our ideas and research. When applicable, we have linked this work to more general literatures such as those pertaining to story-telling and to griefwork. In this final chapter, we shall describe what we see as the limitations of our approach. We shall also describe future directions for theory and research.

WHEN ACCOUNT-MAKING MAY NOT BE BENEFICIAL: THE CASE OF INCOMPREHENSIBLE TRAUMA

A question that the astute reader may have asked from the very beginning is, "Is account-making *always* beneficial for the human grappling with major psychic issues?" We have argued in our theoretical model and elsewhere in this book that account-making in general is beneficial to the re-establishment of a sense of control, the quest for purpose in one's life or in one's survival, and in self-identity affirmation. However, we would accept that there may be exceptions. The study of Holocaust victims and victims of other such horrific events, which are beyond the comprehension of all persons except those who survive them, suggests such exceptions.

One dictionary definition of "survivor" is a person who continues living or existing after or in spite of an event that inflicts personal loss. In the case of the Holocaust survivors, the term "existing" may more appropriately describe the psychic state that continues for many years beyond the event. Why? Because the experience involved such enormous dehumanization, brutalization, degradation, and devastation in general that cognitively dealing with it creates unbearable psychological pain (and other negative emotions such as guilt in surviving when so many did not). To talk, or even think, about the event may be excruciatingly demoralizing. To return to the key account-making sub-process of "working-through" (described in chapter 3), the survivor may have survived by numbing and otherwise blocking and resisting any outpouring of emotions, and for some period after the event may have an aversion to examining his or her memories of the event and their meanings and implications. This intolerance for remembering may first be manifest toward others: several respondents in a survey of grieving responses among the elderly (see chapter 5) reported that they "try not to think about" their losses and resent it when *others* "insist on whining about their own grief." The emotions and suffering tied to those memories are so great as to preclude any conscious, intentional meddling with them. They may, however, be represented in dreams or subsconsciously influential in various ways in the individual's life.

Beyond the personal suffering that may be encountered on reviewing and remembering these events, it may be the case that close others either cannot cope with the survivor's report of the events (especially repeated over time), or they are shut out completely from the review and cathartic activity. As one combat veteran of the Vietnam War said, "I carried on like that [not talking to others] for the last 20 years. If people tried to get too close, I just shut 'em off" (an anonymous veteran's report in 'The Forever War,' in *Star Magazine*, 18 June 1989). Klein-Parker (1988) provides a telling discussion of the attitudes of adult children of Holocaust survivors toward their parents. She indicates that a frequent report of these children was "I know nothing about my parents." Instead of learning about the histories of their parents first hand from their parents, these children typically learned about their parents' histories to some degree, and the Holocaust in general, from the reports of non-family members and from books and other written materials. Concomitantly, these adult children reported that their parents had difficulty relating to feelings like love and affection. As one said, "When I show emotions, my father's response has been, you have to be strong, you get yourself together. He had become stoic as a result of the Holocaust. It is difficult for him to show my sister and me any affection" (Klein-Parker, 1988, p. 203). As we argued in chapter 3, central to account-making and the communication of accounts is emotion associated with the contents of the account. What we are concluding here is that because the events were so powerful, many years later survivors still cannot bear that emotion, even with professional help such as psychotherapy. Indeed, simple existence may seem to dictate that the lid be kept shut tight on these emotions.

On the other hand, the survivor may feel that he or she cannot communicate with others about the trauma, either because they do not care or cannot bear the emotional burden of listening and becoming empathically involved. One such survivor told a reporter of his attempt to facilitate his recuperation and gain some perspective by revisiting the site of the concentration camp in which he had been incarcerated as a youth (article by Jim Pollock, in *Des Moines Register*, 16 July 1989). He described the journey as unfolding like a gloomy, unsettling dream. At the concentration camp site, he asked a woman to take his picture, and she walked away without a word. "He began spilling out his memories to some people, and he 'just broke down. I couldn't do it, so I just kept on walking'" (p. 2E). This survivor also reported an experience common among survivors, namely a recurrent nightmare involving the original trauma and oneself as a helpless participant: "It's always the same dream . . . . The same killings, dogs barking at you and biting you, getting chased, and all the beatings. The same old scream for help, and nobody there" (ibid.).

Is it any wonder that the account-making experience – either in private thought or in conversation with friends or loved ones – may be too painful for some to embark on? The painful impact by strong implications often extends to loved ones anyway. Klein-Parker (1988) reports that many of her respondents, themselves children of survivors, stated that they had experienced the same nightmares as their parents: "A common dream depicted scenes of being on cattle trains as they were transported to the camps. Vivid imagery of the Holocaust terrors was reported over and over again" (1988, p. 210). It may be that some of these survivors are merely "existing," and not living life in a full and enhancing way. But we would be quick to contend that it is not our right to judge what is psychologically possible given the enormity of some traumas. Mere psychological existence, in these instances, may represent a miraculous feat.

So, we have duly noted what may be a major exception to the tendency of survivors to gain psychological strength through account-making activity. Frankl (1963) and others who have coped with trauma by account-making and reporting to others, and, in some cases, crusading to tell the story to all the world of the events and their human toll, represent but one end of a continuum. This is the end with which we have been most fascinated in telling our story in this book, but by our focus we have not meant to deny its opposite extreme.

We do believe that the "tellers" and "crusaders" have often performed a great service by modeling the power of the human will to create purpose and hope for others who must follow in their steps. Their accounting activity and that of their loved ones should be given greater attention by scholars interested in account-making. In *Fireflies*, which we described earlier in this book, the author, Morrell, notes that the story he will tell with "terrible compulsion" is the most dreadful thing that ever happened to him. A similarly crusading mother of a teenage girl, who had been murdered by her boyfriend, makes the following point in describing her long-term effort to establish victims' rights and counseling groups: "I was really driven to try and tell Jenny's story so that someone else could be saved. It gives me a sense of 'I'm doing this for Jenny'" (*Des Moines Register*, 23 July 1989, p. 7B).

The gruesome 1969 Tate–LaBianca murders, committed in Los Angeles by members of the Manson "family," present a continuing stimulus for wonder about the extent to which humans can display cruelty toward other humans. Doris Tate, mother of Sharon Tate, has dedicated her life to making certain that the story of the murders is not forgotten and the convicted murderers are not paroled from prison. She offers this insight into her enduring vigilance: "I am the victims' voice . . . . How can you go on with your life when you're totally consumed with this? . . . Something deep down inside of me keeps saying, 'Why do human beings react so violently with no reason? Why kill people they don't even know?'" ('The Murders they'll never forget' *Chicago Tribune*, 6 August 1989, Sunday Commentary, p. 51).

As a final illustration of this motivation to crusade or otherwise act to provide greater meaning for significant loss, Sara Andrews, the mother of a twenty-four-year-old woman murdered in Chicago in 1984, has found solace by writing a book-length manuscript about her daugher's life, in which she depicts her daughter's involvement in drugs and in the "fast lane" of Chicago nightlife prior to her death. Andrews indicates that the writing has helped ease the pain: "I had to go through the pain . . . . You start inside. You want that touchstone of pain – from her to me. You take the pain into yourself. You ingest it, you purge yourself and you justify. Maybe she didn't feel anything. Maybe she was drugged . . . '" (Jon Anderson, 'Searching for Marcy,' *Chicago Tribune*, 30 April 1989, p. 4, section 5).

So for some survivors and their close others, the telling of the story of the trauma and the search for its causes become a "magnificent obsession." The account-making activity itself gives meaning to life and the will to go on. In general, however, these ideas are speculative. A notable shortcoming of work to date on stress, account-making, and coping is that we are only just beginning to develop useful conceptual approaches, and still far too little relevant empirical work has been done.

THE ROLE OF THE SELF IN ACCOUNT-MAKING

We have given attention to the role of the self in the accounting process at various points in our presentation, including our emphasis on the possibility of identity change as a part of account-making in response to severe stress. None the less, our coverage is still marginal in terms of the specifics of operation for so critical a component of account-making. This omission needs to be corrected in future work. The topic of the self is re-emerging as one of the most inviting focal points in social psychology in the 1980s and 1990s. Important new insights on the self have been provided in recent works, including those by Wicklund and Gollwitzer (1982), Wicklund and Braun (1987), Baumeister (1986, 1989), Wegner (1989), and Wegner and Vallacher (1986).

There are also many classic, penetrating analyses of the nature of self that deserve renewed consideration by accounts researchers. We have noted the value of self-disclosure work for the accounts arena (e.g. Derlega, Wilson, and Chaikin, 1976). Depth of public account-making is probably influenced greatly by disclosure variables, such as gender of other, reciprocity, and trust. As another example, Altman and Taylor's (1973) social penetration model of relationship development continues to have a major impact on our understanding of how people get to know one another. This process involves "penetrating through" others' layers of identity from the most superficial (e.g. color of eyes) to the most central (e.g. deeply-held beliefs and personality tendencies). Self-disclosure is the currency for such penetration, and it may be theorized that in close relationships, partners are simultaneously engaged in the process of deepening their knowledge of other. How accounts may be forged tactically so as both to protect against penetration and penetrate these layers represents a type of inquiry ripe for investigation (see discussion of accounts as persuasion below, p. 149).

What implications may be found in contemporary work on the self for our analysis of account-making? Baumeister's (1986) life-interpretation theory is most relevant since this conception is concerned with people's needs for meaning in their lives. In general, he argues that people's presentations of themselves in the form of their autobiographical narratives represent the product of negotiation between the self and the external world, and that the actual events are edited to fit a script that suits the goals of the self. That is, people use these narratives to reconcile their experiences with their self-concepts. Baumeister suggests that people have needs for purpose, efficacy, justification, and self-worth. As this theory implies, the establishment of these meanings is the chief work of the self, and one is unfulfilled to the extent that these needs for meaning are unmet. We would suggest that there may be considerable interplay between such needs and a person's unfolding master-account. For example, a person's account may not only contain the types of needs for meaning identified by Baumeister, but may also provide associative bonds and contextual background for these needs. The account may show how such needs have differential importance to the individual, depending on the issue. Family stories, for example, may emphasize the endurance of family character through adversity. Or, as another illustration, an individual's post-break-up account may be formulated to conclude that "It was worth the pain to learn that I am worthwhile in my own right," or "Life goes on but I will never forget my one great love." The need for meaning, then, may express itself in courage, or grief, or melodrama.

ACCOUNT-MAKING AS PERSUASION

Another fascinating direction that our treatment of accounts has largely ignored concerns the extent to which account-making is a persuasive endeavor. We discussed the self-presentational motivation for account-making in chapter 1 and noted an individual's need to convince self of the credence of one's accounts. However, we have provided little insight into the dynamics of the influence process. Do people often persuade others with their accounts by appeal to the logic of their arguments (cf. Petty and Cacioppo's (1986) concept of a central route to persuasion)? Do they also appeal to others via their attractiveness, style of presentation, and apparent sincerity (that is, via so-called the peripheral route)? It seems possible that the accounts and person-perception research format described in chapter 4 may have promise for investigating these persuasion processes as they are influenced by account-making.

How does the process work in group settings? Are certain kinds of groups subject to "groupthink," to use Janis's (1982) influential concept? According to this idea, the members of groups (for example, the Watergate break-in conspirators) may exhibit a distorted style of thinking that renders group members incapable of reason or realism. Groupthink usually involves an unreasonably optimistic illusion about how important the group is and its potential influence. It involves a skewing in information-gathering not unlike that found in egocentrically-oriented individuals whose central focus is on how to maintain or enhance self-interests. Janis indicates that groupthink is "a mode of thinking that people engage in when they are deeply involved in a cohesive in-group, when the members' strivings for unanimity override their motivation to realistically appraise alternative courses of action" (1982, p. 9). To Janis, groupthink is a disease-like process that makes groups inefficient and possibly immoral in their behavior. A vital characteristic of groupthink is that of close-mindedness. (Janis uses the term "mindguarding".) We believe that accounts-type evidence would provide a good reading on the depth and extent of groupthink within an organization. The individual group members' accounts of important group-culture events should coincide both with one another and with the overarching account of the organization's *raison d'être*. (See McCauley (1989) for a recent analysis of groupthink.) Group members may communicate (or conspire to develop) a shared or convergent account of their shared history. Depending on the group's nature (e.g. university committee, family, social club) and agenda (e.g. social or task-focused), members may strive to keep their individual accounts in tacit consensus with the 'master' story or collective theme.

ACCOUNT-MAKING AND CLOSE RELATIONSHIPS

Our interest in the accounts topic derived from our work on close relationships. The close relationship area remains ripe for work on account-making. One direction concerns different conceptions of love. Styles of loving – for example, the erotic style is conceived to involve a quick, intense form of loving, which emphasizes considerable physical contact – is a topic that has stimulated considerable research in recent years (e.g. Lee, 1973; Hendrick and Hendrick, 1986, 1989; Davis and Latty-Mann, 1987). We might ask whether people who exhibit these different personality styles also show different account-making tendencies in their courting and close-relating activities.

Perhaps more relevant to the account-making topic is the work by Mills and Clark on communal love (e.g. Mills and Clark, 1982, 1986). They conceptualize a major distinction between communal and exchange relationships. Exchange relationships are exemplified by relationships between acquaintances or business associates. In these relationships, the giving or taking of one thing in return for another is followed. That is, a standard of *quid pro quo* obtains in exchange relationships. In communal relationships, however, each person feels a special responsibility, and usually a special desire, to be concerned with others' welfare. Communal relationships are exemplified by relationships between friends, family, and lovers or romantic partners. In other words, communal relationships appear to follow the "norm of mutual responsiveness" (Pruitt, 1972), with each party exhibiting sensitivity to when particular benefits would be most helpful to their partners or loved ones.

Do people engage in different types of account-making in communal love relationships compared to exchange relationships? They probably do. In fact, it is likely that people engage in considerable account-making prior to the development of communal relationships. This account-making may pertain to one's love for other, other's special and endearing qualities, and other's worthiness as a condition for sacrificing one's own resources in order to make the other feel happy. Beyond the developmental stage, accounts are usually most pronounced when communal relationships start to deteriorate. In such situations, the self-defensive and other-blaming orientations described in chapter 2 may often be manifest in the accounts produced. The proposed general principle would be, where the stakes are high in close relationships, as in communal relationships, the need for explanation associated with any major actions would also appear to be high. Further, within such a relationship, explanation and account-making may be stimulated most at the beginning and end-stages of the relationship. To our knowledge, this line of reasoning has not been empirically evaluated in previous work on communal relationships. But given the compelling literature that is developing on communal relationships, such an idea would seem to be timely for future examination.

OTHER NAGGING QUESTIONS AND FUTURE CHALLENGES

Operational Definition and Artifacts

We have attempted to develop our version of accounts in such a way that an account may be operationally defined and reliably measured. In chapter 1, we have discussed the present state of the art of methodology and have provided some perspective on enhancement of the measurement process. However, knowing the operational boundaries of a story or an account seems to be very different from knowing the operational boundaries of, say, an attitude, an emotion, or even a thought. To say that it involves a "package" of something, whether thoughts or feelings or whatever, may imply that the concept goes beyond the bounds of what can readily be quantified and measured in social psychology. We agree that the concepts of accounts and account-making may not be for the faint of heart in scientific social psychology. But we would also argue that the complex constituents of an account are, in principle, no more insuperable for empirical analysis than the complex constituents we now know to be a part of the attitude. Some of the recent research described in this book attests to this point. Most important, the molar aspect of the accounts concept is central to its identity. *To reduce the account to an attribution, or even several disconnected attributions, is to miss the value of studying the more complex entity of the account.*

A related set of qualms pertains to artifact issues. One is that people have little awareness of their own cognitive operations (e.g. Nisbett and Wilson, 1977). Another is that asking people to report accounts is necessarily a reactive procedure; that is to say, research participants may "develop" a report on the spot, but not have given the matter much thought prior to the request – a criticism reminiscent of questions raised early in the history of attitudes research. These are legitimate concerns and must be properly weighed in accounts research. There are, however, some rejoinders that mitigate the impact of such concerns. As for the dilemma of what peple know about their own cognitive operations, it is unclear that such an issue should reduce the potential value of the contents of their reports on their thoughts and/or thinking processes. It is our task as scholars to develop ideas about how and why those thoughts were composed and about their implications for behavior. It is enough, we would claim, for a research participant to have and be willing to report a story, without knowing the cognitive procedures involved in the formulation of the story. Indeed, the very availability of a reportable story – so near, as it were, to the surface – represents an important matter worthy of research in itself.

On the issue of reactivity, researchers may be able to ease that worry somewhat by the use of diaries and/or continuous report devices. As an example of the latter type of device, "beeping" participants to report thoughts and feelings at certain times, as used by Csikszentmihalyi (1982) and colleagues (see discussion below, pp. 154–5) has yielded useful information. The Rochester Interaction Record, which involves a daily behavioral self-report by participants, has proved to be a valuable research tool for activity (e.g. Nezlek, Wheeler, and Reis, 1983). As yet another possibility, researchers may seek reports from others who are close to the participants, thereby attempting to gain corroboration about the contents of accounts. Moreover, it simply is not cogent to believe that elaborate stories about why a marriage ended, for example, are fabricated simply to satisfy the appetite of a researcher.

Care in evaluating the type of account requested is vital to the research enterprise. Account-making, by definition, is a retrospective enterprise. With the effort of developing a story, perception and meaning may change relative to the point before the development of the story began. Furthermore, it might be expected that people will review many aspects of events associated with important problems of living and revise their stories about these events over time. Story-telling may also be edited in the very act of telling the story. These possibilities notwithstanding, they represent quite different issues from the claim that the story did not exist in some form prior to the request for an account. Few if any forms of research on psychological processes can be easily implemented without some recourse to self-report evidence (Harvey, Hendrick, and Tucker, 1988). In accounts research, that assertion is especially true, and scholars should not apologize for the need. They should, though, *be cautious about the meaning* of the collected data, both for their theories and in terms of representing a veridical report of the participant's accounts and other thoughts, feelings, and experiences.

Causal Directions

We have collected no data that definitively establish accounts' causal role in social psychological phenomena. How critical is that absence? Research involving longitudinal designs is needed to measure and test the operation of accounts and account-making in important social psychological phenomena. Such a step can help answer the question of causal direction. What we have at present is a fair case of circumstantial evidence about the role of accounts in various domains (e.g. in close relationship maintenance and dissolution). This state of affairs is not unusual for phenomena that are complex and close to our real-life struggles. Even as work on the causal aspects of attribution and marital satisfaction has progressed by quantum leaps in recent years (e.g. Fincham and Bradbury, in press), it seems possible that the accounts concept will be examined in more sophisticated ways and found to play a role in many important phenomena in the future. As described in chapter 4, despite over three decades of research on person perception, it is only recently that the idea of accounts as stimulus presentations has been introduced and found to be useful.

Accounts Themes, Other Psychological States and Behavior

An imposing topic, which was touched on in chapter 3, concerns the association between account themes, psychological states (such as one's holding certain emotions or attitudes), and patterns of behavior. In chapter 3, we placed special emphasis upon the importance of examining account-making and social interaction episodes in the context of personal problems and stress. As Mead (1932) suggested, in social interaction, interpretation of ongoing action is shaped continually by our reconstructed past and our future projects. For Mead, "Durations are a continual sliding of presents into each other. The present is a passage constituted by processes whose earlier phases determine in certain respects their later phases" (1932, p. 28). This continual process is what Mead refers to as emergence, which means that a definition of a situation is progressively open to transformation over time and circumstance.

We would argue that in order for the conceptual and research domain of accounts to be of value to social scientists, it is critical to establish discernible associations among people's stories and the process of developing them, other psychological states, and related lines of behavior and interaction with others. For example, does one's perception of an abandonment theme in one's account ("All my lovers seem to have left me for someone they find more needy") affect one's self-insights and/or determination to break the pattern, for instance, by being more demanding – or even more independent? Empirical evidence only hints at such linkages, even as the relationships among attribution, other psychological states, and behavior have received only scant attention (Sillars, 1981; Yarkin, Harvey, and Bloxom, 1981; Allen et al., 1987). Certainly, theory and available evidence do point to associations between accounts and expectations for behavior (see Harvey, Agostinelli, and Weber, 1989). As suggested in chapter 3, accounts may lead people to hold cognitive expectations about others (possibly stereotypes) and act toward them in ways consistent with those sets.

We need theoretical and empirical work that addresses relationships between account-making and quality of life in general and coping with stress in particular. The latter has been discussed in chapter 3, but what about the possible associations between accounts and quality of life? Some of the most interesting work today in social and personality psychology derives from Mihaly Csikszentmihalyi's program of research on his theory of what is involved in optimal experience in work and leisure (e.g. Csikszentmihalyi, 1982; Csikszentmihalyi and LeFevre, 1989). He contends that optimal experience is the bedrock of existence. He calls optimal experience *flow*. It is the subjective reality that justifies the actions and events of a person's life history. Without it, there would be no purpose in living, working, and relating. Flow is conceived to be determined by factors, such as the levels of affect and potency accompanying experience (one's epiphanies, to use Campbell's (1972) term) and by cognitive efficiency and motivation. The latter factors are similar to White's (1959) notion of competency motivation and how it is positively related to people's level of satisfaction in many areas of life.

We would propose that the ideas of flow or optimal experience and competency motivation may be usefully related to account-making; it is likely that for some types of events (e.g. grieving, coping with major loss), flow and quantity and depth of account-making are highly positively related. For other types of events (e.g. beginning dating), they may be inversely related. As with so many other possible integrations in the account-making field, this one awaits exploration but promises much. That promise may be especially true in terms of close relationship events where either one needs to do a lot of account-making, or possibly it may get in the way of spontaneity, as in the early dating case. In severe stress sequences, it may be postulated that account-making will serve as an antidote to attempted escape from felt pressure by means of drugs, plunging into depression, or even suicide. In a sense, account-making in such circumstances may facilitate return to a flow of optimal experience. (See Cskszentmihalyi (1975) for an analysis rich with such implications.)

Returning to the accounts–action association, we also need archival probes of the possibility that specific themes in accounts are linked to concrete forms of action (such as the possibility that the "witchcraft" theme was used to justify witch-hunts in medieval Europe and even early modern America, and which led to the slayings of many eccentric but quite innocent women and men; or more recent "witch-hunts" for communists in post-war America). Either accounts may precede such behavior, or people may first behave toward others and then formulate accounts for their actions via self-perception processes (Bem, 1972). As argued in chapters 3 and 4, this critical linkage between action and account-making must receive focal attention in future research on accounts. World events offer fascinating prospects for such work through archival analysis. History is often revised according to political and other agendas. The Soviet Union's official line on the Hungarian leader Imre Nagy is a case in point. He was tried and executed after he resisted the Soviet invasion of Hungary in 1956. In the late 1980s, however, a new administration came to power in the USSR, and posthumously Nagy was declared a martyr and hero. Hungarians were allowed to give Nagy a funeral with honor in 1989, symbolizing this new reading (and writing) of history.

Accounts researchers may be able more comprehensively to elucidate accounts and how they change over time by investigating such episodes in archival studies. Furthermore, as is true with attributional processes and other social psychological processes (e.g. Moscovici, 1984; Billig, 1987; Hewstone, 1989) the domain of accounts research will be more telling and relevant to social life when it is broadened to address the role of cultural factors and how account-making may differ cross-culturally. In western cultures, for example, literality is a more important quality in chronicles than seems true of more allegorical values in eastern traditions. This is evident in the issue of "fundamentalism" regarding religious scripture. Do such value differences extend to individuals' life-stories and accounts?

A set of promising possibilities for studying psychological correlates of account-making is suggested by Pennebaker (1984, 1989) and colleagues' research (see related discussion in chapter 3). Across several correlational studies, these researchers have found that *not confiding about any type of traumatic event* is associated with illness episodes and measures of subjective distress (Pennebaker, 1989). Although the exact nature and circumstances of this confiding in natural settings are not fully described in this work, it would appear that the experience bears much similarity to sharing one's account with a significant other. These investigators have asked their research participants to provide fragments of accounts during in-person interviews. Ingeniously, Pennebaker and his associates have examined tone of voice, handwriting, and skin conductance as correlates of confiding behavior in the laboratory setting. They have found that each of these indices has differentiated the parts of accounts that did involve traumatic detail from those that did not (thus, participants began to whisper and accelerate their tape-recorded speech or change their handwriting from cursive to block lettering when they were referring to traumatic moments). Pennebaker and colleagues also found that these tendencies are related to certain personality factors, such as negative affectivity (Watson and Clark, 1984). They have suggested that such tendencies reflect a "letting go" or disinhibition, which may accompany the lifting of social or cognitive constraints against self-disclosure of highly sensitive information.

For future work on account-making, it is inviting to consider whether the same types of non-verbal tendencies found by Pennebaker and colleagues might occur when people are reporting different types of stories under different types of conditions. For example, these tendencies might be studied while individuals are reporting their accounts to a close other versus a stranger or persons of different gender or age (see also the research by Giles, Williams, and Coupland, in press, that was mentioned in chapter 3, as involving a similarly interesting format for investigating the occurrence of talk about various topics under differing sociolinguistic conditions). Or is it not likely that one's handwriting and/or voice qualities in reporting an account about a trauma might vary as a function of the nature of the audience (as is implied in our discussion of audience factors in chapter 1)?

Accounts and Person Perception Schemata

In chapter 4, we have outlined the beginning of a program of research on accounts and person-perception. But in real life, how do people use account-making in *forming* impressions of others, or in managing impressions others obtain of them? Certainly, in long-term relationships, partners typically provide one another with in-depth presentations of key stories in their lives. With strangers, or short-term acquaintances, however, we may develop only the rudimentary framework of extensive stories. Yet, we may elaborate on these trait inferences based on those brief fragments. In describing his own tendency to elaborate, Steven Soderbergh the writer and director of the 1989 award-winning film 'sex, lies, and videotape,' says: "Soon after I meet someone, I wonder what kind of relationships they have: Are they the dominant person? I usually construct a whole story about their private life" (Gene Siskel, in Arts Section, *Chicago Tribune*, 6 August 1989, p. 6).

A new idea about account-making may be necessary to understand this latter process. It may be helpful to think of *account gists* as those fragments that for most people who meet countless others in the course of life, perforce fill our memories. The gist has all of the elements of a story – character, plot, lines, and so on – without as much detail or completeness. We believe that it is more than a cognitive schema involving some type of categorization with attending expectation. These gists may be important in defining action and person-perception patterns. What we can dredge up over time from our "knowledge base" of many, many other human beings will be such gists, and they may effectively determine what we think about or do toward those people.

As humans we possess many gists that are less directly related to action but that, nevertheless, in their cumulative and informing ways, color our perceptions of and actions toward people in general. Thus, a basic reality of account-making in life is that one can best know only his or her own story, and very well the stories of only a handful of close, highly significant others over the lifespan. How else could it be? To know much about self alone is already a formidable task, but to know *many* others' stories, and to know *well* how they feel about those stories – their meanings, implications for living, etc., would be a herculean task even for a person who makes a living listening to others' stories (e.g. a psychotherapist). Hence, the study of gists may be just as important in the ways one understands many types of others as is the study of accounts for understanding oneself and close others.

A NOT-SO-FINAL WORD

It seems difficult to conclude our discussion of accounts in this book (albeit ours is a brief presentation, and has not attempted to be global or exhaustive) with any conclusive or final language. Our very topic, the account as we conceive it and as it has fascinated us, is far more process than product. In the ongoing business and creative call of account-making, does one ever reach the point of inscribing 'Finis,' and setting aside for the last time the cognitive pen? We think not. We suggest rather that the account, like the very relationships it examines and chronicles, does not end, but goes on, continuing at other levels of action and consciousness: an enduring memorial, an unending analysis. Just as the account is too vital and emotionally potent to be a mere souvenir, so too our treatment of accounts and account-making here represents not the conclusion of our interest but, we hope, the beginning of a discussion.

We have enjoyed the luxury of monopolizing the forum, but we have missed the dynamics of debate. We have represented and echoes some collegial concerns about such issues as definition, veridicality, methodology, and measurement, and have tried to anticipate other questions that might give pause to otherwise interested scholars. We have sought to present these issues accurately, but are strongly motivated to portray the phenomena of accounts and account-making in a naturally intriguing and inviting light. We have found these stories people tell – after preserving memories, enhancing themes, and examining consciences – to offer, as with a ready, open hand, a richness of information and nuance about life-experience. Here are to be found such qualities as anguish, pathos, melodrama, dismissal, and deceit. These stories are recorded, retold, and transmitted to style impressions, cope with intense grief, and instruct beloved pupils. The stories say, "I made it," "I'll never get over him," "I'm not like her," "I'll never forget, nor forgive," and "You are the image of your grandmother!" They inspire, motivate, depress, anger, and exhilarate.

But they do not end. And so we do not conclude our discussion here. We continue it with other work, in other arenas, and we hope with new interest among readers we meet through our writing here. The accusation has been made of us that accounts are our 'passion.' That seems a fair and apt impression with which now to leave the reader as we invite further exploration into the fascinating enterprise of account-making.

SUMMARY

We have come to the end of our journey in providing our conception of the social psychology of account-making. The present chapter noted some of the major limitations of work to date. Included in the discussion was the question of when account-making may not be beneficial; the unexplored roles of the self in account-making; how account-making may be a form of persuasion; issues of operationalization, causal direction, linkages with various psychological states, behavior, and social interaction; and how account-making and person perception may work in real life. We have introduced the idea of account gists as a way of depicting the fragmentary story-understanding possessed by people of the many others in their lives about whom they have only modest information. The difficulty of entertaining great scope and depth about many accounts, including one's own, also was noted. Finally, we noted our own passion for the study of accounts and hope that some of that sentiment has been passed on to the reader.

Notes

1 In our design, we attempted to make the stimulus person similar to our respondent to enhance identification with the stimulus person. We checked this assumption by asking respondents, 'How similar do you feel to the presenter?' (a seven-point scale accompanied the question). Then, in all of the analyses, we statistically controlled for any variance due to perceived lack of similarity.

1 It is remarkable how many works on grief and griefwork make reference to re-entering or attending to the "everyday" world of "day-to-day" existence. A suggestion running through such allusions is that the recent griever has stepped *out* of time or out of step with the real or social world, experiencing his or her pain and confusion in slow motion, working to gain sufficient energy and running start to re-enter the mainstream or orbit of mundane but essentially vital existence. This may also emerge in the tone of unreality or suspended animation evident in many written and spoken accounts.

2 Elderhostel participant, UNCA, in response to a survey on coping with close relationship loss.

3 "Recovery" is in quotes here because, as Rando (1988) observes, recovery from loss is a relative accomplishment, rather than an absolute state. The same qualification applies to "resolving" grief.

4 Elderhostel student, responding to survey on coping with close relationship loss.

5 Ibid.

6 Ibid.

7 Ibid.

8 Ibid.

9 Ibid.

10 Elderhostel respondent.

11 Ibid.

12 Ibid.

13 Names and locations have been changed.

CHAPTER 7 ACCOUNTS IN LITERARY FORM

1 Thanks to Kathleen Nilan, Department of History, University of North Carolina at Asheville, for the translation.

2 In Felleman (1936, p. 550).

3 Ibid., p. 554

References

Abramson, P. R. (1984) *Sarah: A sexual biography*, Albany: State University of New York Press.

Albreacht, T. L. and Adelman, M. B. (eds) (1987) *Communicating Social Support*, London: Sage.

Allen, J. L., Walker, L. D., Schroeder, D. A., and Johnson, D. E. (1987) 'Attributions and attribution behavior relations: The effect of level of cognitive development,' *Journal of Personality and Social Psychology*, 52, 1099–109.

Allen, K. R. and Picket, R. S. (1987) 'Forgotten streams in the family life course,' *Journal of Marriage and the Family*, 49, 517–26.

Altman, I. (1989) *Close Relationships in Polygamous Families: An Ecological Analysis*. Address given to second Iowa Conference on Personal Relationships, Iowa City, Iowa.

Altman, I. and Taylor, D. (1973) *Social Penetration*, New York: Holt, Rinehart & Winston.

Altman, I. and Werner, C. (eds) (1985) *Home environments. Vol. 8 human behavior and environment,* New York: Plenum.

Antaki, C. (1987) 'Types of accounts within relationshps.' In R. Burnett, D. Clark, and P. McGhee (eds), *Accounting for Relationships*, London: Methuen.

Antaki, C. (ed.) (1988) *Analyzing Everyday Explanation*, Beverly Hills, CA: Sage.

Antaki, C. (1989) 'Structured causal beliefs and their defence in accounts of student political action,' *Journal of Language and Social Psychology*, 8, 39–48.

Armstrong, C. (1988) *White Light*, New York, Morrow.

Arnston, P. and Droge, D. (1987) 'Social support in self-help groups: The role of communication in enabling perceptions of control.' In T. L. Albrecht and M. B. Adelman (eds) *Communicating Social Support*, Newbury Park, CA: Sage, pp. 148–71.

Associated Press (1989). "Film to profile Bergman's parents." Stockholm, Sweden, September 2.

Bartlett, F. C. (1932) *Remembering: A study in experimental and social psychology*, New York: Cambridge University Press.

Baumeister, R. F. (1986) *Identity: Cultural Change and the Struggle for Self*, New York: Oxford University Press.

Baumeister, R. F. (1989) *Masochism and the Self*, Hillsdale, NJ: Larence Erlbaum.

Baxter, L. A. (1987) 'Symbols of relationship identity in relationship cultures,' *Journal of Social and Personal Relationships*, 4, 261–80.

Baxter, L. A. and Wilmot, W. (1985) 'Taboo topics in close relationships,' *Journal of Social and Personal Relationships*, 2, 253–69.

Beattie, A. (1986) *Where You'll Find Me*, New York: Linden Press.

Beck, A. T. (1967) *Depression: Clinical, Experimental, and Theoretical Aspects*, New York: Harper & Row.

Bellah, R. N., Madsen, R., Sullivan, W. M., Swidler, A., and Tipton, S. (1985) *Habits of the Heart: Individualism and Commitment in American Life*, Berkeley: University of California Press.

Bem, D. J. (1972) 'Self-perception theory.' In L. Berkowitz (ed.), *Advances in Experimental Social Psychology*, Vol. 6. New York: Academic Press, pp. 1–62.

Berger, C. R. (1988) 'Planning, affect, and social action generation.' In R. L. Donohew, H. Sypher, and E. T. Higgins (eds), *Communication, Social Cognition, and Affect*, Hillsdale, NJ: Erlbaum, pp. 93–116.

Berger, C. R. (1979) 'Beyond initial interaction: Uncertainty, understanding, and the development of interpersonal relationship.' In H. Giles and R. N. St. Clair (eds), *Language and Social Psychology*, Oxford: Basil Blackwell, pp. 122–44.

Berger, C. R. and Bell, R. A. (1988) 'Plans and the initiation of social relationships,' *Human Communication Research*, 15, 217–35.

Bergman, M. S. and Jucovy, M. E. (eds) (1982) *Generations of the Holocaust*, New York: Basic Books.

Bernikow, L. (1987) *Alone in America*, New York: Harper & Row.

Berscheid, E. (1983) 'Emotion.' In H. H. Kelley, E. Berscheid, A. Christensen, J. Harvey, T. Huston, G. Levinger, E. McClintock, L. A. Peplau, and L. A. Peterson, (eds), *Close Relationships*, San Francisco: Freeman, pp. 110–68.

Billig, M. (1987) *Arguing and Thinking: A Rhetorical Approach to Social Psychology*, Cambridge: Cambridge University Press.

Birren, J. E. (1987) 'The best of all stories,' *Psychology Today*, May, pp. 91–2.

Blumstein, P. W. et al. (1974) 'The honoring of accounts,' *American Sociological Review*, 39, 551–566.

Bradbury, T. and Fincham, F. C. (in press) 'Attribution in marriage: review and critique,' *Psychological Bulletin*.

Breier, A. (in press) 'Long-term effects of early parental loss,' *Archives of General Psychiatry*.

Brende, J. S. and Parson, E. R. (1985) *Vietnam Veterans: The roads to recovery*, New York: Plenum Press.

Brown, R. and Kulik, J. (1977) 'Flashbulb memories,' *Cognition*, 5, 73–99.
Bruner, J. (1987) 'Life as narrative,' *Social Research*, 54, 11–32.
Bruner, J. (1989) *Folk Psychology*. Address at Biennial Meeting of the Society for Research in Child Development, Kansas City.
Bulmer, M. (1979) 'Concepts in the analysis of qualitative data,' *Sociological Review*, 27, 651–77.
Burke, K. (1945) *A Grammar of Motives*, New York: Prentice Hall.
Burnett, R. (1987) 'Reflection in personal relationships.' In R. Burnett, P. McGhee, and D. D. Clarke (eds) (1987) *Accounting for Relationships*, London: Methuen, pp. 74–93.
Burnett, R., McGhee, P. and Clarke, D. C. (eds) (1987) *Accounting for Relationships*, London: Methuen.
Cacioppo, J. T. and Petty, R. E. (1982) 'The need for cognition,' *Journal of Personality and Social Psychology*, 42, 116–31.
Campbell, J. (1972) *Myths to Live By*, New York: Bantam.
Campbell, J. (interview with Bill Moyers) (1988) *The Power of Myth*, ed. B. S. Flowers, New York: Doubleday.
Carbaugh, D. (1988) *Talking American: Cultural Discourses on Donahue*, Norlwood, NJ: Ablex.
Clarke, D. (1987) 'Emotion, decision and the long-term course of relationships.' In. R. Burnett, P. McGhee, and D. D. Clarke (eds), *Accounting for Relationships*, London: Methuen, pp. 3–21.
Cochran, L. (1985) *Position and the Nature of Personhood*, Westport, CT: Greenwood Press.
Cochran, L. (1986) *Portrait and Story*, Westport, CT: Greenwood Press.
Cochran, L. and Claspell, E. (1987) *The Meaning of Grief*, Westport, CT: Greenwood Press.
Cody, M. J. and McLaughlin, M. L. (1985) 'Models for the sequential construction of accounting episodes: Situational and interactional constraints on message selection and evaluation.' In R. L. Street and J. N. Cappella (eds), *Sequence and Pattern in Communicative Behavior*, London: Edward Arnold, pp. 50–69.
Cody, M. J. and McLaughlin, M. L. (in press) 'Interpersonal accounting.' In. H. Giles and P. Robinson (eds), *The Handbook of Language and Social Psychology*, London: John Wiley.
Cohen, E. A. (1988) *Human Behavior in the Concentration Camp*, London: Free Association Books.
Coles, R. (1986) *The Moral Life of Children*, Boston, MA: Atlantic Monthly.
Coles, R. (1989) *The Call of Stories*, Boston, MA: Houghton Mifflin.
Colwin, L. (1981) *The Lone Pilgrim*, New York: Alfred A. Knopf.
Colwin, L. (1982) *Family Happiness*, New York: Alfred A. Knopf.
Cooley, C. H. (1902) *Human Nature and the Social Order*, New York: Scribner's.

Couch, C. J. and Weiland, M. W. (1986) 'A study of the representative-constituent relationship.' In C. Couch (ed.), *Studies in Symbolic Interaction*, Greenwich, CT: JAI Press, pp. 375–91.

Coupland, N., Coupland, J., Giles, H., and Henwood, K. (1988) 'Accommodating the elderly: Invoking and extending a theory,' *Language in Society*, 17, 1–41.

Cross, A. (1986) *No Word from Winifred*, New York: Ballantine.

Csikszentmihalyi, M. (1975) *Beyond Boredom and Anxiety*, San Francisco: Jossey-Bass.

Csikszentmihalyi, M. (1982) 'Toward a psychology of optimal experience.' In L. Wheeler (ed.), *Review of Personality and Social Psychology*, 3, Beverly Hills: Sage, pp. 13–26.

Csikszentmihalyi, M. and LeFevre, J. (1989) 'Optimal experience in work and leisure,' *Journal of Personality and Social Psychology*, 56, 815–22.

Darley, J. M. and Fazio, R. H. (1980) 'Expectancy confirmation process arising in the social interaction sequence,' *American Psychologist*, 35, 867–81.

Davis, K. E. and Latty-Mann, H. (1987) 'Love styles and relationship quality: A contribution to validation,' *Journal of Social and Personal Relationships*, 4, 409–28.

Davis, M. H. (1983) 'Measuring individual difference in empathy,' *Journal of Personality and Social Psychology*, 44, 113–26.

Davison, P. (1989) 'The passing of Thistle,' *Atlantic Monthly*, Vol. 264, No. 3, September, p. 71.

Derlega, V. J., Margulis, S. T., and Winstead, B. A. (1987) 'A social psychological analysis of self-disclosure in psychotherapy,' *Journal of Social and Clinical Psychology*, 5, 205–15.

Derlega, V. J., Wilson, M., and Chaiken, A. L. (1976) 'Friendship and disclosure reciprocity,' *Journal of Personality and Social Psychology*, 34, 578–82.

Duck, S. (1987) 'Adding apples and oranges: Investigation implicit theories about personal relationships.' In R. Burnett, P. McGhee, and D. C. Clarke (eds) *Accounting for Relationships*, London: Methuen, pp. 215–24.

Duck, S. (1988) *Relating to Others*, Chicago: Dorsey.

Duck, S. and Sants, H. K. A. (1983) 'On the origin of the specious: Are personal relationships really interpersonal states?' *Journal of Social and Clinical Psychology*, 1, 27–41.

Ephron, N. (1983) *Heartburn*, New York: Alfred A. Knopf.

Erikson, E. (1963) *Childhood and Society*, 2nd edition, New York: W. W. Norton.

Felleman, H. (1936) *Best Loved Poems of the American People*, New York: Doubleday.

Fincham, F. D. and Bradbury, T. N. (in press) 'Cognition in marriage: A program of research on attributions.' In D. Perlman and W. Jones (eds), *Advances in Personal Relationships*, Vol. 2, Greenwich, CT: JAI Press.

Fisher, C. (1987) *Postcards from the Edge*, New York: Simon & Schuster.

Fiske, S. T. and Taylor, S. E. (1984) *Social Cognition*, Reading, MA: Addison-Wesley.

Fletcher, G. J. O. (1983) 'The analysis of verbal explanations for marital separation: Implications for attribution theory,' *Journal of Applied Social Psychology*, 13, 245–58.

Fletcher, G. J. O., Danilovics, P., Fernandez, G., Peterson, D., and Reeder, G. D. (1986) 'Attributional complexity: An individual differences measure,' *Journal of Personality and Social Psychology*, 51, 875–84.

Folkes, V. S. (1982) 'Communicating the reasons for social rejection,' *Journal of Experimental Social Psychology*, 18, 235–52.

Frankl, V. E. (1956) *Man's Search for Meaning*, New York: Washington Square.

Garfinkel, H. (1956) 'Conditions of successful degradation ceremonies,' *American Journal of Sociology*, 61, 420–24.

Garfinkel, H. (1967) *Studies in Ethnomethodology*, Englewood Cliffs, NJ: Prentice Hall.

Gazzaniga, M. S. and Le Doux, J. E. (1978) *The Integrated Mind*, New York: Plenum.

Gergen, K. J. and Davis, K. E. (eds) (1985) *The Social Construction of the Person*, New York: Springer-Verlag.

Gergen, K. J. and Gergen, M. M. (1983) 'Narratives of the self.' In T. R. Sarbin and K. E. Scheibe (eds), *Studies in Social Identity*, New York: Praeger, pp. 254–72.

Gergen, K. J. and Gergen, M. M. (1984) 'The social construction of narrative accounts.' In K. Gergen and M. Gergen (eds), *Historical Social Psychology*, Hillsdale, NJ: Lawrence Erlbaum.

Gergen, K. J. and Gergen, M. M. (1987) 'Narratives of relationship.' In R. Burnett, P. McGhee, and D. C. Clarke (eds) *Accounting for Relationships*, London: Methuen, pp. 269–315.

Giles, H., Williams, A., and Coupland, N. (in press) 'Communication, health and the elderly: Frameworks, agenda and a model.' In *Health, and the Elderly* (Fulbright Colloquia Serial No. 8), Manchester: Manchester University Press.

Ginsburg, G. P. (1988) 'Rules, scripts and prototypes in personal relationships.' In S. Duck (ed.), *Handbook of Personal Relationships*, New York: John Wiley, pp. 23–39.

Glick, I. O., Weiss, R. S., and Parkes, C. M. (1974) *The First Year of Bereavement*, New York: John Wiley.

Goffman, E. (1959) *The Presentation of Self in Everyday Life*, Garden City, NY: Doubleday-Anchor Books.

Goffman, E. (1971) *Relations in Public*, New York: Basic Books.

Greenberg, I. and Greenberg, B. (1979) 'Telling your children about the Holocaust,' *Kosher Home's Jewish Living*, March/April, New York:

Adar Communications.

Greene, B. (1989) 'Jason's friend died; friendship didn't,' *Chicago Tribune*, May 14, p. 5–1.

Greenwald, A. G. (1980) 'The totalitarian ego: Fabrication and revision of personal history,' *American Psychologist*, 35, 603–18.

Harré, R. (1977) 'The ethogenic approach: Theory and practice.' In L. Berkowitz (ed.), *Advances in Experimental Social Psychology*, Vol. 10, Academic Press, New York.

Harré, R. (1979) *Social Being: A theory for social psychology*, Oxford: Basil Blackwell.

Harré, R., Clarke, D., and DeCarlo, N. (1985) *Motives and Mechanisms*, New York: Methuen.

Harré, R. and Secord, P. F. (1972) *The Explanation of Social Behavior*, Oxford: Basil Blackwell.

Harvey, J. H., Harris, B., and Barnes, R. D. (1975) 'Actor–observer differences in the perceptions of responsibility and freedom,' *Journal of Personality and Social Psychology*, 32, 22–8.

Harvey, J. H., and Smith, W. P. (1977) *Social psychology: An attributional approach*, St. Louis: C. V. Mosby.

Harvey, J. H., Wells, G. L., and Alvarez, M. D. (1978) 'Attribution in the context of conflict and separation in close relationships.' In J. H. Harvey, W. Ickes, and R. F. Kidd (eds), *New Directions in Attribution Research*, Vol. 2, Hillsdale, NJ: Lawrence Erlbaum, pp. 235–59.

Harvey, J. H., Harris, B., and Lightner, J. M. (1979) 'Perceived freedom as a central concept in psychological theory and research.' In L. C. Perlmuter and R. A. Monty (eds), *Choice and Perceived Control*, Hillsdale, NJ: Lawrence Erlbaum, pp. 275–300.

Harvey, J. H., Yarkin, K. L., Lightner, J. M., and Town, J. P. (1980) 'Unsolicited interpretation and recall of interpersonal events,' *Journal of Personality and Social Psychology*, 38, 551–68.

Harvey, J. H., Weber, A. L., Yarkin, K. L., and Stewart, B. (1982) 'An attributional approach to relationship breakdown and dissolution.' In S. Duck (ed.), *Dissolving Personal Relationships*, Vol. 4, London: Academic Press, pp. 107–26.

Harvey, J. H., Flanary, R., and Morgan, M. (1986) 'Vivid memories of vivid loves gone by,' *Journal of Social and Personal Relationships*, 3, 359–73.

Harvey, J. H., Weber, A. L., Galvin, K. S., Huszati, H. C., and Garnick, N. N. (1986) 'Attribution and the Termination of close relationships: A special focus on the account,' In R. Gilmour and S. Duck (eds), *The Emerging Field of Personal Relationships*, Hillsdale, NJ: Lawrence Erlbum, pp. 189–201.

Harvey, J. H., Hendrick, S. S., and Tucker, K. (1988) 'Self-report methods in the study of personal relationships.' In S. Duck and W. Ickes (eds), *Handbook of Research on Personal Relationships*, New York: John Wiley, pp. 99–113.

Harvey, J. H., Turnquist, D. C., and Agostinelli, G. (1988) 'Identifying attributions in oral and written explanations.' In C. Antaki (ed.), *Analyzing Everyday Explanation: A casebook of methods*, London: Sage, pp. 32–42.

Harvey, J. H., Agostinelli, G., and Weber, A. L. (1989) 'Account-making and formation of expectations about close relationships.' In C. Hendrick (ed.), *Review of Personality and Social Psychology*, 10, 39–62.

Harvey, J. H., Orbuch, T. L., and Weber, A. L. (1990) 'A social pscyhological model of account-making in response to severe stress.' *Journal of Language and Social Psychology*.

Hasselstrom, L. M. (1989) *Windbreak*, Berkeley, CA: Barn Owl Books.

Heider, F. (1958) *The Psychology of Interpersonal Relations*, New York: John Wiley.

Hendrick, C. and Hendrick, S. (1986) 'A theory and method of love,' *Journal of Personality and Social Psychology*, 50, 392–402.

Hendrick, C. and Hendrick, S. S. (1989) 'Research on love: Does it measure up?' *Journal of Personality and Social Psychology*, 56, 784–94.

Hewstone, M. (1989) *Causal Attribution: From Cognitive Processes to Collective Beliefs*, Oxford: Basil Blackwell.

Hill, C. T., Rubin, Z., and Pelau, L. A. (1976) 'Breakups before marriage: The end of 103 affairs,' *Journal of Social Issues*, 32, 147–68.

Hobfoll, S. E. (1989) 'Conservation of resources: A new attempt at conceptualizing stress,' *American Psychologist*, 44, 513–24.

Holtzworth-Munroe, A. and Jacobson, N. J. (1985) 'Causal attributions of married couples,' *Journal of Personality and social Psychology*, 48, 1389–412.

Horowitz, M. J. (1986) *Stress response syndromes* (2nd ed.), Northvale, N. J.: Jason Aronson.

Hovland, C. I., Janis, I. L., and Kelley, H. H. (1953) *Communication and Persuasion*, New Haven, CT: Yale University Press.

Hunt, M. (1969) *The Affair: A Portrait of Extra Marital Love in Contemporary America*, New York: World Publishing.

Huston, T. L., Surra, C. A., Fitzgerald, N. M., and Cate, R. M. (1981) 'From courtship to marriage: Mate selection as an interpersonal process.' In S. Duck and R. Gilmour (eds), *Personal Relationships 2: Developing personal relationships*, London: Academic Press, pp. 53–88.

Ickes, W. Bissonnette, V., Garcia, S., and Stinson, L. (1990) 'Implementing and using the dyadic interaction paradigm,' *Review of Personality and Social Psychology*, 11, 16–44.

Jacobson, N. S., McDonald, D. W., Follette, W. C., and Berley, R. A. (1985) 'Attributional processes in distressed and nondistressed married couples,' *Cognitive Therapy and Research*, 9, 35–50.

Janis, I. L. (1982) *Victims of Groupthink*, 2nd edition, Boston, BA: Houghton-Mifflin.

Janoff, Bulman, R. and Frieze, I. H. (1983) 'A theoretical perspective for understanding reactions to victimization,' *Journal of Social Issues*, 39, 1–17.

Janoff-Bulman, R. and Wortman, C. B. (1977) 'Attributions of blame and coping in the "real world?" Severe accident victims react to their lot,' *Journal of Personality and Social Psychology*, 35, 351–63.

Jaynes, J. (1976) *The Origin of Consciousness in the Break-down of the Bicameral Mind*, Boston, MA: Houghton-Mifflin.

Jellison, J. M. (1977) *I'm Sorry I Didn't Mean to, and Other Lies we Love to Tell*, New York: Chatham Square.

Jones, E. E. and Davis, K. E. (1965) 'From acts to dispositions: The attribution process in personal perception.' In L. Berkowitz (ed.), *Advances in Experimental Social Psychology*, Vol. 2, New York: Academic Press.

Jones, E. E. and Pittman, T. S. (1982) 'Toward a general theory of strategic self-presentation.' In J. Suls (ed.), *Psychological Perspectives on the Self*, Hillsdale, NJ: Lawrence Erlbaum, pp. 231–62.

Jourard, S. M. (1971) *Self-disclosure*, New York: John Wiley.

Joyce, J. (1916). *Dubliners*. New York: Penguin Books.

Kavesh, L. and Lavin, C. (1989) 'You can be too pretty, too young, and love hurts,' *Chicago Tribune*, May 17, p. 2–2.

Keen, S. (1988) 'The stories we live by,' *Psychology Today*, December, 43–6.

Kelley, H. (1983) 'Perceived causal structures.' In J. Jarpars, F. D., Fincham, and M. Hewstone (eds), *Attribution Theory and Research: Conceptual, Developmental and Social Dimensions*, London: Academic Press, pp. 843–69.

Kelley, H., Bersheid, E., Christensen, A., Harvey, J., Huston, T., Levinger, G., McClintock, E., Peplau, A. and Peterson, D. (1983) *Close Relationships*, San Francisco: Freeman.

Kingma, D. R. (1987) *Coming Apart: Why Relationships End and How to Live Through the Ending of Yours*, Berkeley, CA: Conari Press.

Klein-Parker, F. (1988) 'Dominant attitudes of adult children of Holocaust survivors toward their parents.' In J. P. Wilson, Z. Harel, and B. Kahana (eds), *Human Adaptation to Extreme Stress*, New York: Plenum.Klinger, E. (1977) *Meaning and Void*, Minneapolis: University of Minnesota Press.

Klinger, E. (1977) *Meaning and void,* Minneapolis: University of Minnesota Press.

Kohout, F., Berkman, L., Evans, D., and Cornoni-Huntley, J. (1983) *Psychological Assessment Devices Adopted for Population Surveys of the Elderly: Two new forms of the CES-D*. Paper presented at the Annual meeting of the Public Health Association, Dallas, TX.

Koller, A. (1982) *An Unknown Woman: A Journey to Self-Discovery*, New York: Bantam.

Kranzler, E. (1988) Personal communication regarding predictors of children's ability to cope with grief.

Kubler-Ross, E. (1969) *On Death and Dying*, New York: Collier Books.

Langer, E. J. and Rodin, J. (1976) 'The effects of choice and enhanced personal responsibility for the aged: A field experiment in an institutional setting,' *Journal of Personality and Social Psychology*, 34, 191–8.

Lawson, A. (1988) *Adultery: an analysis of love and betrayal*, New York: Basic Books.

Lazarus, R. S. (1966) *Psychological Stress and the Coping Process*, New York: McGraw-Hill.

Le Carré, J. (1989) *The Russia House*, New York: Alfred A. Knopf.

Lee, J. A. (1973) *The Colors of Love: An exploration of the ways of loving*, Don Mills, Ont: New Press.

Lefebvre, R. E., and Sanford, S. L. (1985) 'A multi-modal questionnaire for strain,' *Journal of Human Stress*, 11, 69–75.

Lerner, M. J. (1980) *The Belief in a Just World: A fundamental delusion*, New York: Plenum Press.

Levinger, G. (1977) 'Re-viewing the close relationship.' In G. Levinger and H. L. Raush (eds), *Close Relationships*, Amherst, MA: University of Massachusetts Press.

Lewin, K. (1935) 'The conflict between Aristotelian and Galilean modes of thought in contemporary psychology.' In *A Dynamic Theory of Personality*, New York: McGraw-Hill, p. 1–43.

Lewis, C. S. (1963) *A Grief Observed*, New York: Bantam Books.

Lichtman, R. R. and Taylor, S. E. (1986) 'Close relationships of female cancer patients.' In B. L. Andersen (ed.), *Women with Cancer*, New York: Springer-Verlag, pp. 233–56.

Lifton, R. J. (1988) 'Understanding the traumatized self.' In J. P. Wilson, Z. Harel, and B. Kahana (eds), *Human Adaptation to Extreme Stress*, New York: Plenum Press, p. 7–31.

Lopata, H. Z. (1988) 'Support systems of American widowhood,' *Journal of Social Issues*, 44 (3), 113–28.

Lukacs, J. (1970) *The Passing of the Modern Age*, New York: Harper & Row.

Lyman, S. M. and Scott, M. B. (1970) *A Sociology of the Absurd*, New York: Appleton-Century-Crofts.

Maddi, S. R. (1970) 'Search for meaning,' *Nebraska Symposium on Motivation*, 28, 137–86.

Mancuso, J. C. and Sarbin, T. R. (1983) 'The self-narrative in the enactment of roles.' In T. R. Sarbin and K. E. Scheibe (eds), *Studies in Social Identity*, New York: Praeger, pp. 233–53.

Mandler, G. (1964) 'The interruption of behavior,' *Nebraska Symposium on Motivation*, 12, Lincoln: University of Nebraska Press, pp. 163–220.

Mandler, J. M. (1984) *Stories, Scripts, and Scenes: Aspects of schema theory*, Hillsdale, NJ: Lawrence Erlbaum.

Markus, H. (1977) 'Self-schemata and processing information about the self,' *Journal of Personality and Social Psychology*, 35, 63–78.

Marmar, C. R. and Horowitz, M. J. (1988) 'Diagnosis and phase-oriented treatment of post-traumatic stress disorder.' In J. P. Wilson, Z. Harel, and B. Kahana (eds), *Human Adaptation to Extreme Stress*, New York:

Plenum Press, pp. 81–103.
Masheter, C., and Harris, L. M. (1986) 'From divorce to friendship: A study of dialectic relationship development,' *Journal of social and Personal Relationships*, 3, 177–89.
Matthews, S. H. (1986) *Friendship Through the Life Coruse: Oral Biographies in Old Age*, Beverly Hills, CA: Sage.
McAdams, D. P., (1980) 'A thematic coding system for the intimacy motive,' *Journal of Research in Personality*, 14, 413–32.
McAdams, D. P. (1982) 'Intimacy motivation.' In A. Stewart (ed.), *Motivation and Society*, San Francisco: Jossey-Bass, pp. 133–71.
McCall, G. J. and Simmons, J. L. (1978) *Identities and Interactions*, New York: Free Press.
McCauley, C. (1989) 'The nature of social influence in groupthink: Compliance and internalization,' *Journal of Personality and Social Psychology*, 57, 250–60.
McClelland, D. C. (1986) 'Some reflections on the two psychologies of love,' *Journal of Personality*, 54, 334–53.
McFarland, C. and Ross, M. 91987) 'The relation between current impressions and memories of self and dating partners,' *Personality and Social Psychology Bulletin*, 13, 228–38.
McGhee, P. (1987) 'Postword: The idea of the account and future research.' In R. Burnett, P. McGhee, and D. Clarke (eds), *Accounting for Relationships*, London: Methuen, pp. 321–32.
McLaughlin, M. L., Cody, M. J., and O'Hair, H. D. (1983) 'The management of failure events: Some contextual determinants of accounting behavior,' *Human Communication Research*, 9, 209–24.
Mead, G. H. (1932) *The philosophy of the present*, Chicago: University of Chicago Press.
Mead, G. H. (1934) *Mind, Self, and Society*, Chicago: University of Chicago Press.
Metts, S. (1989) 'An exploratory investigation of deception in close relationships,' *Journal of Social and Personal Relationships*, 6, 159–79.
Miller, G. A., Galanter, E., and Pribram, K. H. (1960) *Plans and the Structure of Behavior*, New York: Holt, Rinehart and Winston.
Miller, I. (1987) *Burning Bridges: Diary of a Midlife Affair*, New York: G. P. Putnam's Sons.
Mills, C. W. (1940) 'Situated actions and vocabularies of motive,' *American Sociological Review*, 5, 904–13.
Mills, J. and Clark, M. S. (1982) 'Exchange and communal relationships.' In L. Wheeler (ed.), *Review of Personality and Social Psychology*, Vol. 3, Beverly Hills, CA: Sage, pp. 121–44.
Mills, J., and Clark, M. S. (1986) 'Communications that should lead to perceived exploitation in communal and exchange relationships,' *Journal of Social and Clinical Psychology*, 4, 225–34.
Monat, A., and Lazarus, R. S. (eds) (1977) *Stress and Coping*, New York: Columbia University Press.

Moos, R. H. (ed.) (1986) *Coping with Life Crises*, New York: Plenum Press.

Morrell, D. (1988) *Fireflies*, New York: E. P. Dutton.

Moscovici, S. (1984) 'The phenomenon of social representations.' In R. M. Farr and S. Moscovici (eds), *Social Representations*. Cambridge: Cambridge University Press.

Murray, E. J., Lamnin, A. D., and Carver, C. s. (1989) 'Emotional expression in written essays and psychotherapy,' *Journal of Social and Clinical Psychology*, 4, 414–29.

Myerhoff, B. (1978) *Number our Days*, New York: Touchstone.

Myerhoff, B. (1982) 'Life history among the elderly: Performance, visibility, and remembering.' In J. Ruby (ed.), *A Crack in the Mirror: Reflective perspectives in anthropology*, Philadelphia: University of Pennsylvania Press, pp. 1–35.

Neisser, U. (1976) *Cognition and Reality*, San Francisco: Freeman.

Neisser, U. (1982) 'Snapshots or benchmarks.' In U. Neisser (ed.), *Memory Observed: Remembering in natural contexts*, San Francisco: Freeman, pp. 43–8.

Newman, H. (1981) 'Communication within ongoing intimate relationships: An attribution perspective,' *Personality and Social Psychology Bulletin*, 7, 59–70.

Nezlek, J., Wheeler, L., and Reis, H. T. (1983) 'Studies of social participation.' In H. T. Reis (ed.), *Naturalistic Approaches to Studying Social Interaction*, San Francisco: Jossey-Bass, pp. 57–73.

Nisbett, R. E. and Wilson, T. D. (1977) 'Telling more than we can know: Verbal reports on mental processes,' *Psychological Review*, 84, 231–59.

Oliner, S. P. and Oliner, P. M. (1988) *The Altruistic Personality*, New York: Free Press.

Orbuch, T. L. (1988) *Responses to and Coping with Nonmarital Relationship Terminations*. Unpublished doctoral dissertation, University of Wisconsin-Madison.

Orbuch, T. L., Harvey, J. H., and Russell, S. M. (1989) 'Account-making and person perception.' Manuscript in preparation.

Orvis, B. R., Kelley, H. H., and Butler, D. (1976) 'Attributional conflict in young couples.' In J. H. Harvey, W. J. Ickes, and R. F. Kidd (eds), *New Directions in Attribution Research*, Vol. 1, Hillsdale, NJ: Lawrence Erlbaum, pp. 353–86.

Osgood, C. (1962) 'Studies on the generality of affective meaning systems,' *American Psychologist*, 17, 10–28.

Pagis, D. (1989) 'Ein Leben,' *The New Yorker*, April 3, p. 85.

Palmer, L. (1987) *Shrapnel in the Heart*, New York: Random House.

Parkes, C. M. (1972) *Bereavement: Studies of Grief in Adult Life*, New York: International Universities Press.

Pennebaker, J. W. (1985) 'Traumatic experience and psychosomatic disease: Exploring the roles of behavioral inhibition, obsession, and confining,' *Canadian Psychology*, 26, 82–95.

Pennebaker, J. W. (1989) 'Confession, inhibition, and disease.' In L. Berkowitz (ed.), *Advances in Experimental Social Psychology*, Vol. 22, Orlando: Academic Press, pp. 211–44.

Peplau, L. A. (1983) 'Roles and gender.' In H. H. Kelley, E. Berscheid, A. Christensen, J. H. Harvey, T. L. Huston, G. Levinger, E. McClintock, L. A. Peplau, and D. R. Peterson (eds), *Close Relationships*, New York: Freeman.

Petty, R. E. and Cacioppo, J. T. (1986) *Communication and Persuasion: Central and peripheral routes to attitudes change*, New York: Springer-Verlag.

Pruitt, D. G. (1972) 'Methods for resolving differences of interest: A theoretical analysis,' *Journal of Social Issues*, 28, 133–54.

Prus, R. C. (1975) 'Resisting designation: An extension of attribution theory into a negotiated context,' *Sociological Inquiry*, 45, 3–14.

Radner, G. (1989) *It's Always Something*, New York: Simon & Schuster.

Rando, T. A. (1988) *Grieving: How to Go On Living When Someone You Love Dies*, Lexington, MA: Lexington Books.

Read, S. J. (1987) 'Constructing causal scenarios: A knowledge structure approach to causal reasoning,' *Journal of Personality and Social Psychology*, 52, 288–302.

Robbe-Grillet, A. (1986) *The Art of Fiction*, The Paris Review, XCI, 46.

Romine, D. (1989) 'Styron's choice: Author tells his story of depression so others won't have to survive it alone,' *Chicago Tribune*, July 3, pp. 1–2.

Rosenblatt, P. C. (1983) *Bitter, Bitter, Tears*, Minneapolis: University of Minnesota Press.

Rosenblatt, P. C. (1988) 'Grief: The social context of private feelings,' *Journal of Social Issues*, 44(3), 67–78.

Ross, M. (1988) *Memory in Social Context*. Paper presented at meeting of the American Psychological Association, Atlanta, Gerogia, August.

Ross, M. (1989) 'The relation of implicit theories to the construction of personal histories,' *Psychological Review*, 96, 341–57.

Ross, M. and Sicoly, F. (1979) 'Egocentric biases in availability and attribution,' *Journal of Personality and Social Psychology*, 37, 322–36.

Rubin, D. C. (ed.) (1986) *Autobiographical Memory*, New York: Cambridge University Press.

Rubin, L. B. (1983) *Intimate Strangers: Men and Women Together*, New York: Harper & Row.

Rubin, Z. and Mitchell, C. (1976) 'Couples research as couples counseling,' *American Psychologist*, 31, 17–25.

Runyan, W. M. (1982) *Life Histories and Psychobiography*, New York: Oxford University Press.

Russell, D., Peplau, L. A., and Cutrona, C. E. (1980) 'The revised UCLA Loneliness Scale: Concurrent and discriminate validity evidence,' *Journal of Personality and Social Psychology*, 39, 472–80.

Sartre, J. P. (1964) *The Words*, New York: Braziller.

Scarf, M. (1980) *Unfinished Business*, New York: Ballatine.

Schachter, S. L. (1959) *The Psychology of affiliation*, Stanford, CA: Stanford University Press.

Schafer, D. E., Berghorn, F. J., Holmes, D. S., and Quadagno, J. S. (1986) 'The effects of reminiscing on the perceived control and social relations of institutionalized elderly,' *Activities, adaptation, and Aging*, 8, 95–110.

Schank, R. C. and Abelson, R. (1977) *Scripts, Plans, Goals and Understanding*, Hillsdale, NJ: Lawrence Erlbaum.

Schinto, J. (1987) 'Private lives,' *Boston Globe*, December 17.

Schlenker, B. R. and Weigold, M. F. (in press). 'Self-identification and accountability.' In R. A. Giacalone and P. Rosenfeld (eds), *Impression management in organizations*. Hillsdale, N.J: Erlbaum.

Schlenker, B. R., Weigold, M. F., and Doherty, K. (in press). 'Coping with accountability.' In C. R. Snyder and D. R. Forsyth (eds), *The handbook of social and clinical psychology*. New York: Pergamon.

Schneider, D. J., Hastorf, A. H., and Ellsworth, P. C. (1979) *Person Perception*, Reading, MA: Addison-Wesley.

Schoenbach, P. (1980) 'A category system for account phases,' *European Journal of Social Psychology*, 10, 195–200.

Schuchter, S. R. (1986) *Dimensions of grief*, San Francisco: Jossey-Bass.

Schwarz, N. and Clore, G. L. (1983) 'Mood, missattribution, and judgments of well-being,' *Journal of Personality and Social Psychology*, 45, 513–23.

Scott, M. B. and Lyman, S. (1968) 'Accounts,' *American Sociological Review*, 33, 46–62.

Seligman, M. E. P. (1975) *Helplessness*, San Francisco: Freeman.

Semin, G. R. and Manstead, A. S. R. (1983) *The Accountability of Conduct: A social psychological analysis*, London: Academic Press.

Shotter, J. (1984) *Social Accountability and Selfhood*, Oxford: Basil Blackwell.

Shotter, J. (1987) 'The social construction of an "us": Problems of accountability and narratology.' In R. Burnett, P. McGhee, and D. D. Clarke (eds), *Accounting for Relationships*, London: Methuen, pp. 225–47.

Sillars, A. L. (1981) 'Attributions and interpersonal conflict resolution.' In J. H. Harvey, W. Ickes, and R. F. Kidd (eds), *New Directions in Attribution Research*, Vol. 3, Hillsdale, NJ: Lawrence Erlbaum, pp. 279–305.

Simons, H. W. (1989) 'Introduction.' In H. W. Simons and T. Melia (eds), *The Legacy of Kenneth Burke*, Madison: University of Wisconsin Press, pp. 3–27.

Simons, H. W. and Melia, T. (eds) (1989) *The Legacy of Kenneth Burke*, Madison: University of Wisconsin Press.

Snyder, C. R., Higgins, R. L., and Stucky, R. J. (1983) *Excuses: Masqueradee in Search of Grace*, New York: John Wiley.

Snyder, M. and Swann, W. B. (1978) 'Behavioral confirmation in social interaction: From social perception to social reality,' *Journal of Experimental Social Psychology*, 14, 148–62.

Snyder, M., Tanke, E. D., and Berscheid, E. (1977) 'Social perception and interpersonal: On the self-fulfilling nature of social stereotypes,' *Journal of Personality and Social Psychology*, 35, 656–66.

Snyder, M. L. and Wicklund, R. A. (1981) 'Attribute ambiguity.' In J. H. Harvey, W. Ickes, and R. F. Kidd (eds) *New Directions in Attribution Research*, Vol. 3, Hillsdale, NJ: Lawrence Erlbaum, pp. 197–221.

Staudacher, C. (1987) *Beyond Grief*, Oakland, CA: New Harbinger Publications.

Steinbergh, J. W. (1988) *A Living Anytime*, Boston, MA: Troubadour Press.

Stone, E. (1988) *Black Sheep and Kissing Cousins: How our family stories shapes us*, New York: Times Books.

Stryker, S. (1981) 'Symbolic interactionism: Themes and variations.' In M. Rosenberg and R. H. Turner (eds), *Sociological Perspectives on Social Psychology*, New York: Basic Books.

Surra, C. A. (1985) 'Courtship types: Variations in interdependence between partners and social networks,' *Journal of Personality and Social Psychology*, 49, 357–75.

Svetvilas, K. (1989) 'Suicide silence: Denial hurts survivors,' *Iowa City Press Citizen*, July 8, p. 1A.

Sykes, G. M. and Matza, D. (1957) 'Techniques of neutralization: A theory of delinquency,' *American Sociological Review*, 22, 664–70.

Tait, R. and Silver, R. C. (1989) 'Coming to terms with major negative life events.' In J. S. Uleman and J. A. Bargh (eds), *Unintended Thought*, New York: Guildford, pp. 351–82.

Tatelbaum, J. (1980) *The Courage to Grieve*, New York: Harper & Row.

Taylor, S. E. and Schneider, S. K. (1989) 'Coping and the simulation of events,' *Social Cognition*, 7, 174–94.

Taylor, S. E., Wood, J. V., and Lichtman, R. R. (1983) 'It could be worse: Selective evaluation as a response to victimization,' *Journal of Social Issues*, 39, 19–40.

Tetlock, P. E. and Boettger, R. (1989) 'Accountability: A social magnifier of the dilution effect,' *Journal of Personality and Social Psychology*, 57, 388–98.

Thompson, S. C. (1981) 'Will it hurt less if I can control it?' *Psychological Bulletin*, 90, 89–101.

Thompson, S. C. and Janigian, A. S. (1988) 'Life schemes: A framework for understanding the search for meaning,' *Journal of Social and Clinical Psychology*, 7, 260–80.

Toth, S. A. (1981) *Blooming*, Boston, MA: Little, Brown.

Toth, S. A. (1984) *Ivy Days: Making My Way Out East*, Boston, MA: Little, Brown.

Toulmin, S. E. (1958) *The Structure of Argument*, Cambridge: Cambridge University Press.

Town, J. P. and Harvey, J. H. (1981) 'Self-disclosure, attribution, and social interaction,' *Social Psychology Quarterly*, 44, 291–300.

Trabasso, T. and van den Broek, P. (1985) 'Causal cohesion and story cohesion.' In H. Mandl, N. L. Stein, and T. Trabasso (eds), *Learning and the Comprehension of Discourse*, Hillsdale, NJ: Lawrence Erlbaum.

Trabasso, T., van den Broek, P., and Suh, S. Y. (1988) *Logical Necessity and Transitivity of Causal Relations in the Representation of Stories*. Unpublished manuscript, University of Chicago.

Truitt, A. (1982) *Daybook: The Journal of an Artist*, New York: Penguin Books.

Tulving, E. (1983) *Elements of Episodic Memory*, New York: Oxford University Press.

Turnquist, D. C., Harvey, J. H., and Andersen, B. L. (1988) 'Attributions and adjustment of life-threatening illness,' *British Journal of Clinical Psychology*, 27, 55–65.

Tyler, A. T. (1988) *Breathing Lessons*, New York: Alfred A. Knopf.

Updike, J. (1987) *Trust Me*, New York: Ballantine Books.

USA Today (1989). "Personal, but only to a point." February 6, p. 2D.

Vachon, M. L. S. and Stylianos, S. K. (1988) 'The role of social support in bereavement,' *Journal of Social Issues*, 44 (3), 175–90.

Van Sommers, P. (1988) *Jealousy*, New York: Penguin Books.

Vaughan, D. (1986) *Uncoupling: Turning Points in Intimate Relationships*, New York: Oxford University Press.

Viorst, J. (1986) *Necessary Losses*, New York: Fawcett.

Vonnegut, K. (1966) *Mother Night*, New York: Dell.

Walster, E. (1966) 'Assignment of responsibility for an accident,' *Journal of Personality and Social Psychology*, 3, 73–9.

Walster, E., Walster, G. W., and Berscheid, E. (1978) *Equity Theory and Research*, Rockleigh, NJ: Allyn & Bacon.

Warren, R. P. (1989) *New and Selected Essays*, New York: Random House.

Watson, D. and Clark, L. A. (1984) 'Negative affectivity: The disposition to experience aversive emotional states,' *Psychological Bulletin*, 96, 465–90.

Weary, G. and Arkin, R. M. (1981) 'Attributional self-presentation.' In J. H. Harvey, W. Ickes, and R. F. Kidd (eds), *New Directions in Attribution Research*, Vol. 3, Hillsdale, NJ: Lawrence Erlbaum, pp. 223–46.

Weary, G., Harvey, J. H., and Stanley, M. (1989) *Attribution*, New York: Springer-Verlag.

Weber, A. L., Harvey, J. H., and Stanley, M. A. (1987) 'The nature and motivations of accounts for failed relationships.' In R. Burnett, P. McGhee, and D. C. Clarke (eds), *Accounting for Relationships*, London: Methuen, pp. 114–35.

Wegner, D. (1989) *White Bears & Other Unwanted Thoughts: Suppression, Obsession, and the Psychology of Mental Control*, New York: Penguin Books.

Wegner, D. M. and Vallacher, R. R. (1986) 'Action identification.' In R. M. Sorrentino and E. T. Higgins (eds), *Handbook of Cognition and Motivation*, New York: Guildford, pp. 550–82.

Weisman, A. D. (1984) *The Coping Capacity*, New York: Human Sciences Press.

Weiss, R. S. (1975) *Marital Separation*, New York: Basic Books.

Weiss, R. S. (1988) 'Loss and recovery,' *Journal of Social Issues*, 44(3), 37–52.

Weissberg, D. K. (1985) *Children of the Night*, Lexington, MA: Heath.

Wells, G. L. and Gavanski, I. (1988) 'Mental simulation of causality,' *Journal of Personality and Social Psychology*, 56, 161–9.

White, R. W. (1959) 'Motivation reconsidered: The concept of competence,' *Psychological Review*, 1959, 66, 297–333.

Whitman, W. (1982) 'Song of Myself.' In *Complete Poetry and Collected Prose*, New York: The Library of America, p. 246.

Wicklund, R. A. and Gollwitzer, P. M. (1982) *Symbolic Self-completion*, Hillsdale, NJ: Lawrence Earlbaum.

Wicklund, R. A. and Braun, O. L. (1987) 'Incompetence and the concern with human categories,' *Journal of Personality and Social Psychology*, 53, 373–82.

Wilson, J. P., Harel, Z., and Kahana, B. (eds) (1988) *Human Adaptation to Extreme Stress*, New York: Plenum Press.

Winokur, J. (1987) *The Portable Curmudgeon*, New York: The American Library.

Wong, P. T. P. and Weiner, B. (1981) 'When people ask "why" questions, and the heuristics of attributional search,' *Journal of Personality and Social Psychology*, 40, 650–63.

Wortman, C. B. (1975) 'Some determinants of perceived control,' *Journal of Personality and Social Psychology*, 31, 282–94.

Wortman, C. B. and Lehman, D. R. (1985) 'Reactions to victims of life crisis: Support attempts that fail.' In I. G. Sarason and B. R., Sarason (eds), *Social Support: Theory, Research, and Applications*, Dordrecht, The Netherlands: Martinus Nijhoff, pp. 463–89.

Wortman, C. B. and Silver, R. C. (1989) 'The myths of coping with loss,' *Journal of Consulting and Clinical Psychology*, 57, 349–57.

Yarkin, K. L., Harvey, J. H., and Bloxom, B. M. (1981) 'Cognitive sets, attribution, and social interaction,' *Journal of Personality and Social Psychology*, 41, 243–52.

Zeigarnik, B. (1938) 'On finished and unfinished tasks.' In W. D. Ellis (ed.), *A Sourcebook of Gestalt Psychology*, London: Routledge & Kegan Paul.

Index of Subjects

Index of Names

ACA-132C

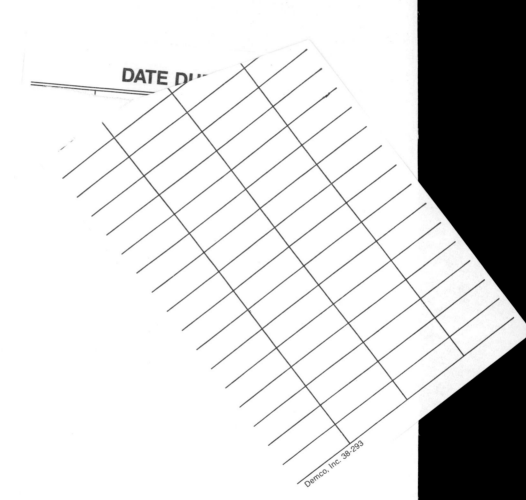

DATE DUE

Demco, Inc. 38-293